# HACKING NORMAL

## By John Stevenot

# TABLE OF CONTENTS

# INTRODUCTION BY TED STEVENOT (JOHN'S DAD)

John Stevenot came into the world on a cloudy midsummer morning in 1990. From the start, he was a special kid. As a newborn, he had radiant blue eyes, and we wondered whether he would be lucky enough to have them keep the color. It turned out he was. How John could look at you with those eyes! It was captivating - like he could see into your soul.

As he grew, John was ahead of his age. He walked early, talked early, and was uncommonly athletic and sports minded. As a toddler, he could throw a ball (and sometimes a baby bottle) with remarkable speed and accuracy. He spent hours swishing basket after basket on his kid-size basketball hoop and, as an early preschooler, he developed the ability to swing a golf club with extraordinary grace.

Throughout his life, John gravitated toward the older kids and the adults. When we used to take miles-long treks at the beach to net blue crabs and fish in the tidal creeks and surf, John always kept up with the "big people" and never complained. In fact, far from it. He couldn't wait to get out there and get fishing!

John was ingrained with a fiery and competitive spirit. At times, this made him a handful to raise. He used to say he hated losing far more than he enjoyed winning. This led to a few post-game drywall repairs over the years. Despite his hot-blooded inclinations, his coaches always loved him. He had an intuitive ability to understand direction and strategy. John never had to be told the play twice. He "got it" and was always a solid contributor to any team.

John carried his intensity and forward outlook into adulthood. He sought advice from mentors and respected leaders. He also read hundreds of books and consumed countless hours of instructional podcasts and videos. As such, he avoided many of the errors in thinking from which so many people needlessly suffer. He habitually questioned the status quo and oriented himself toward the pursuit of higher truth.

His most valued goal was to live life as fully as possible.

While still in college I encouraged him to learn about websites. At the time, he had an interest in "mashup" music, and he started a review site on the topic. He turned out to be a natural in the arena of digital outreach. In no time, his site was throttling my host account and racking up millions of views.

When he graduated from college with honors and a double-major in business, he could have gone to work for any number of great companies. However, I encouraged him to come back home and try to start something of his own. At the time, in addition to my regular business, I was highly involved in grassroots politics. I invited John to help where he could, and he eagerly got involved.

We went on to establish dozens of websites, reach millions and millions of people online, and collect tens of thousands of email subscribers. His early successes with online work eventually inspired John to pursue a career in digital marketing.

Years later, when I finally decided to swear off politics, John did too. Around that same time, and again, in addition to our regular work, John and I started a commercial real estate business that we worked on together part-time. Later, we kicked off a weekly podcast on sales and marketing called, *Sales Prospecting School.* On the show, we discussed various ways to mix old and new-school marketing techniques for effective business development.

During his post college years, John maintained a keen interest in health and exercise. He even got me going back to the gym and in the habit of being in better shape. For several years, John was a CrossFit devotee and frequently took part in local competitions.

On a late-September Saturday in 2018, John tied for his first, first-place finish in a CrossFit competition. Later the same week, we were scheduled to record the 47th episode of our weekly podcast together. Then, without warning, symptoms, or the slightest indication of any ongoing problem, in the early hours of October 5, 2018, John passed away quietly in his sleep.

Just like that...he was gone.

Months later it was determined that the cause of death was an extremely rare and asymptomatic condition impacting the interior of his heart which caused it to stop.

The book you are about to read is based on a manuscript John completed in the summer of 2017. I remember him coming into my office and putting it on my desk soon after it was done. He said, "Well, there it is." I guess I was supposed to proof it for him, but I felt reluctant to do so. We had worked on writing projects together before, and I remember thinking our writing styles were quite different. I didn't want to disturb his way of saying things. So, I left it be.

For a variety of reasons, he never pursued taking the manuscript much beyond that point. I sometimes wonder whether he was depending on me to take it from there. If so, I let him down. It is one of my only regrets from our time together.

Sometime after he died, I got the idea to locate his manuscript and see it through into final book form. During this time, I kept our podcast running on Soundcloud. Even though there weren't any new shows being uploaded, it continued to receive thousands of downloads.

In John's writing, there is a directness and honesty that mirrors his personality. Beyond a few light edits, I made every effort to leave his voice intact. At a few spots, it is not the easiest read and will require the reader's close attention to make the most of it.

However, I find John's raw will to assemble and confer his deepest truisms to the reader to be stirring. Particularly powerful are his exhortations to live fully in the present because *no one knows how much time he or she ultimately has.*

Please enjoy the words and wisdom of this remarkable and beautiful young man! It is my sincere hope that you feel the presence of John's spirit in these pages.

Though John's life ended too soon, I am forever grateful for having known him. He will remain a source of pride and inspiration for me, from now and until the end of my days.

Ted Stevenot

March 2020

# DEDICATION

To all those who believe there is a better
way and to those who believed in me.

"But you see, I have, let's say, sixty years to live. Most of that time will be spent working. I've chosen the work I want to do. If I find no joy in it, then I'm only condemning myself to sixty years of torture. And I can find the joy only if I do my work in the best way possible to me. But the best is a matter of standards – and I set my own standards. I inherit nothing. I stand at the end of no tradition. I may, perhaps, stand at the beginning of one."

– Howard Roark, *The Fountainhead*

# FOREWORD

## THE LADDER

You're standing in a room. The room is illuminated by a white light. On the wall in front of you is painted an extravagant mural, depicting a river with large rocks abruptly protruding from the rushing water. The water seems to bubble and foam as it pushes itself around the hard, grey impediments. On the wall to your right, the mural fades into heavy vegetation. There are trees with vines as thick as a farmer's arm lazily hanging from the branches. Large ferns cover the forest floor.

In the middle of the wall, a fallen tree has been painted coming toward the room. Where the tree ends, a large papier mâché trunk extends into the room. The faux tree makes a small shelter in one corner, where bowls of water and food are neatly stored. On the wall to your left, the mural continues, but constructed here are large faux rocks. Each rock is screwed to the wall in order to give the appearance of a bouldering hill. On the wall behind you there is a door painted with vegetation. Paired with the door is a single, double-sided mirror.

Behind the mirror, scientists are inconspicuously scribbling notes and whispering in hushed voices to each other. In the middle of the room, there is an outline of a small door on the ceiling. The door is held shut by a single, chrome latch that stands out like a firework in the bright blue sky. The floor of the room is littered with branches, plants, and tufts of inedible grass. The strangest thing about this room, however, is the ladder planted in the center. The only life forms inside the room are *five* rhesus monkeys. The scientists, on the other side of the double-sided mirror, are closely observing and recording the behavior of the rhesus monkeys, as the monkeys swing between vines and play upon the ladder.

With a loud bang, the door hidden within the ceiling swings open. A white sleeve emerges and places a bunch of bananas on top of the ladder. The hand retracts back into the ceiling and swings the door shut with a click. The monkeys, frozen from their moment of terror, look around. One monkey cautiously makes his way to the ladder and begins to climb. Each tentative step brings him closer and closer to the bananas. Finally, the *brave* monkey reaches the top of the ladder and glances back down to the others, who are all staring back in bewilderment. The *brave* rhesus monkey reaches out and grabs the bananas.

Suddenly, the light in the room begins flashing blood red, sirens blare, the monkeys start screeching, and the ceiling cascades ice-cold water onto the monkeys. The *brave* monkey drops the bananas, leaps off the ladder. He joins the other monkeys, who are now cowering in terror in the corner under the faux tree trunk. After a moment, the sirens go quiet, the light returns to its vibrant white glow, and only a few residual drops of ice-cold water splash onto the ground.

The monkeys slowly inch their way out from the corner of the room, listening intently for any other signs of danger. All is calm. The *brave* monkey takes a moment to gaze up at the top of the ladder. He can still see the bright yellow fruit shimmering with water under the lights. Before another monkey can beat him to it, he jumps onto the ladder and quickly climbs to the top. He reaches his hand out and grabs the bananas.

Again, the lights turn a blood red, the ceiling rains down ice-cold water, and the sirens ring. Once more, the monkeys rush to cower in the corner. As the room settles, the monkeys look from each other to the bananas. Their heads tilt side to side as they try to understand. They slowly spread back into the room, but this time, none of them race to get the bananas.

Several hours pass and the *brave* monkey is again climbing the ladder in the hope of finally seizing the bananas. The other monkeys notice his attempt to ascend the ladder and begin shrieking. The *brave* monkey ignores their cries and continues to climb. Suddenly, one of the monkeys comes swinging in on a vine and knocks the *brave* monkey off the ladder and to the ground. The *brave* monkey, startled and angry, hisses at the swinging monkey and bounds past him back to the ladder. This time, another monkey tackles him and starts to clobber him with his tiny paws. The other monkeys, who were watching, join in. They bite, hit, and drag the *brave* monkey around the room, leaving specks of blood on the floor and murals. Eventually, the fighting stops. The *brave* monkey sits up, bloodied and beaten. He licks his wounds and limps to the corner opposite of the faux trunk to heal.

The door to the room opens. A man in a white coat picks up the *brave* but injured monkey and carries him out. A few moments later, the door opens again and a woman carries in a new rhesus monkey and sets her on the ground.

This new monkey immediately begins to play. She splashes in the puddles of water and swings from the vines, bounding from one side of the room to the other. The other monkeys only watch. The new monkey notices the ladder in the center of the room and changes course to swing onto it. With one swoop, she lets go of the rope and lands on the bottom step of the ladder. She looks up, sees the bananas, and begins to climb. The four *original* monkeys begin shrieking and running toward the ladder. They quickly climb up and rip the new monkey off the ladder and pummel her into the ground. Just like the *brave* monkey, this new monkey crawls into the corner and tends to her wounds.

The door to the room opens. A man in a white coat enters. This time, however, instead of picking up the injured monkey, he leaves with one of the four remaining *original* monkeys. And, like before, a woman in a white coat comes in with a new rhesus monkey. This new monkey bounds about the room, playing in the water and swinging on the ropes. He, too, begins to climb the ladder toward the easy snack. The other monkeys attack. One monkey even bites off one of the new monkey's fingers. As this violent encounter plays out, the other, injured monkey watches in horror but understands *why*. The new monkey tried to get the bananas.

This time, no one enters the room. There is only a loud bang as the door in the ceiling opens. A white sleeve emerges and removes the bananas from the ladder. Days go by and the two injured monkeys heal.

A few more days pass and the door to the room opens. A man in a white coat takes one of the three remaining *original* monkeys out of the room, leaving only two, while a woman in a white coat leaves behind a brand-new monkey, bringing the total of new monkeys to *three*. Per usual, the new monkey swings around the room, playing on the vines and the ladder. The other monkeys, both new and original, eye this one carefully.

A few hours pass and there is a loud bang. A white sleeve emerges from the ceiling door and places a bunch of bananas onto the ladder. The newest monkey looks up at the bananas and then back at the others. When no one moves, he bounds to the ladder. But, before he can get a paw onto the first step, the *first replacement monkey* tackles him to the floor. She gouges out one of his eyes and begins to jump up and down on his stomach. The other monkeys watch in approval.

After the fight, the injured and partially blinded monkey crawls to the corner to lick his wounds. A man in a white coat enters the room and removes one of the two remaining *original* monkeys. As he leaves, a woman in a white coat leaves behind another new monkey. Again, this new monkey tries to climb the ladder to grab the bananas and the other monkeys take her to the ground with biting and scratching. After the struggle, the wounded monkey crawls to the corner to recover.

After a few moments, the man in the white coat comes in and removes the final *original* rhesus monkey, while the woman leaves behind another new monkey. Like all the others, this new monkey dares to ascend the ladder. And, like all the others, she is ripped from the steps, beaten and bloodied, and then left to heal on her own in the corner. There's a loud bang and a white sleeved arm emerges from the ceiling to remove the bananas. With a click, the yellow fruit is gone.

### Conclusion: "Group Think"

This story has been shared throughout the academic world for decades. It is known as the *5 Monkeys and a Ladder* experiment. If you are concerned about the ethical nature of the story, have no fear. This story is exactly that, *only a story*. It is actually an amalgamation of ideas, inspired by the experiments of G. R. Stephenson, found in "Cultural Acquisition of a Specific Learned Response among Rhesus Monkeys" as well as certain experiments with chimpanzees conducted by Wolfgang Kohler in the 1920s. Over the years, it was pieced together to become the urban legend it is today.

What is most compelling about the story is the learned behavior of each new monkey. Despite never having received the punishment of blaring sirens, blood red light, and cold water, the *new* monkeys still beat up each successive monkey who attempted to climb the ladder to grab the bananas. If it was possible to ask the monkeys (*the new monkeys*) why they acted in such a way, their answer would most likely be, "I don't know. It's just how things are done around here."

This attitude of "it's just how things are done around here" is rampant in many areas of our lives. Most egregiously, it is the dominating mentality that most businesses and employees take when it concerns *work*.

In the following pages, I am going to argue that, like the monkeys, we are battered individuals who have been molded to operate within a work environment that most, if not all, of us do not truly understand. It's a system that fears change to the status quo, also known as what I call *the normal*.

What's worse is that we do not even try to question the system that we operate within because we fear punishment from our peers or superiors. Yet, it is common that our peers also cannot elaborate on why the punishment needs to be administered.

Our reality of work has been established by one, strict definition. And, unfortunately, we have been fed that definition from the moment we were introduced to the idea of work. Because of this, we make massive assumptions about what is *normal* for work, and we staunchly defend those norms. Why, though? Simple. We don't know any different.

## THE ALLEGORY OF THE CAVE

In my meditation class in high school (yes, it was a class and we affectionately called it AP Nap Time), we had to read Plato's famous *Allegory of the Cave*. The allegory is told in three acts: imprisonment in the cave, departure from the cave, and returning to the cave. Each part is crucial to understand because it reveals a basic behavioral pattern within the human condition. Below is a very short, *Cliff Notes*-esque version of the story. As you read the story, reflect on its abridged merits. Try to imagine where in your working life you are the prisoner and where you are the individual who has seen the truth.

### ACT ONE - IMPRISONMENT IN THE CAVE

Plato begins his allegory by asking us to imagine a cave filled with people who have been imprisoned from birth. Therefore, they know no other reality. These prisoners are chained together so that their legs and necks are in a fixed position which forces them to gaze at the wall in front of them. Behind the prisoners is a fire and a raised walkway where other people are carrying objects "of men and other living things" while, at the same time, making various noises. The objects they carry cast shadows onto the wall in front of the prisoners. The noises are the auditory cues that the prisoners associate with each shadow (e.g. a chirp to a bird).

The shadows *are the unquestionable reality* for the prisoners. The shadows are the only reality the prisoners have ever known. The shadows are the only rules, benefits, comforts, and securities that the prisoners have ever experienced. It is very rare that new shadows and animals get introduced because they cause too much discomfort for the prisoners.

*THE PARALLEL TO WORK:*

From childhood, we are inundated with ideas of what it is like to be an adult and work for a company. The shadows we watched dance on the walls were the stories we were told by our parents, teachers and society. Included in those stories were ideas on how to not get fired, how to be a good worker, and how to avoid getting in trouble and losing our jobs.

Most damagingly, we were taught how to achieve success within the confines of those stories. Some of those ideas included: sacrificing our time, playing the *Game of Cubicles*, and climbing the corporate ladder in order to retire rich on the beach with a margarita in hand and sand between our toes. We were never told to question the status quo or look for something different. We were told only to stay the course.

## ACT TWO - DEPARTURE FROM THE CAVE

Plato then supposes that one prisoner is freed. How the prisoner is freed is not important. What is important is that *the prisoner is now looking around him and sees that the shadows are being made by something else*: a fire.

At this point, Plato proposes two courses of action for the freed prisoner. The first (and most likely), is that the prisoner would choose *not to believe his new reality* and would go back to his chains and shadows. He would forget what he saw and remain oblivious to the new information presented to him because it is uncomfortable and scary. The second course of action would be that the freed prisoner, by either choice or force (most likely force because no one wants to willingly up-end their understanding of reality), would walk past the fire toward the entrance of the cave.

Plato says that as the freed prisoner gets closer and closer to the entrance of the cave, sunlight (a metaphor for truth) gets brighter and brighter. At first, the prisoner covers his eyes, but eventually his eyes adjust to the light and he can see a whole new, vibrant world in front of him. He sees the true world, and the true world is more beautiful than the shadows ever were.

*THE PARALLEL TO WORK:*

In my experience, this departure only comes when a mentor or new responsibility calls on a person to question his or her situation. A mentor who sees potential in an individual can persuade that person to question and slowly change his or her environment. Oftentimes, this is done through books or demonstration.

The second type of departure comes from the force of having to deal with a new responsibility (e.g. kids, position, or reassignment – a.k.a. firing). In either situation, the worker has been given the opportunity to seek out something new and better for his life, but it is up to the individual to take the necessary steps in order to realize and appreciate this new way of operating within the norms of society.

## ACT THREE - RETURN TO THE CAVE

Here's where the story gets interesting. Plato continues, saying that the freed prisoner, because of this new knowledge of beauty and reality, would pity his past chain-mates. He would want to bring the news of this better reality back to them. With glee and enthusiasm, the freed prisoner runs back into the dark.

At this moment, two things happen. First, the man cannot see within the cave. His eyes are no longer accustomed to the dark and shadows (curse of knowledge). He fumbles through the caves, grasping for help from the walls (inability to relate). The other prisoners, who have now been disturbed by all the racket, are staring at the freed prisoner in astonishment. The second thing that happens is that the freed prisoner begins to herald the beauty that he has discovered and that if the others want to see this beauty, they only must "throw off their chains." The problem, though, is that he is yelling at the walls and appears to have gone mad with blindness.

The prisoners, being stuck in their shadowy reality, *reject* the freed prisoner. They fear both the uncertainty of what he speaks and the crippling blindness (caused by the light) of the freed prisoner. They do not realize that it is the truth that the freed prisoner is accustomed to, not the lies perpetrated in the dark. Therefore, the words spoken by the freed prisoner fall on deaf ears. The prisoners question what beauty there could be outside the cave. All they have ever seen is the light from the fire and the dancing of the shadows. The prisoners conclude that the "truth" has irreparably harmed the freed prisoner and that they should not undertake a similar journey.

Plato ends his allegory with a bold and damning accusation. Plato believes that the prisoners would then try to kill the messenger because darkness and shadows are the only world they know and ever *want* to know.

*THE PARALLEL TO WORK AND THIS BOOK:*

The point of this book is to give me the opportunity to herald the beautiful world that I have discovered. The problem is many people see me as blind and naive. These people see the ideas that you are about to read as both impossible and impractical. To that, I can only say: *Maybe they are, but have you tried them?* Are you so content with your situation, your *reality*, that you are unwilling to question it? If so, that's fine. But I hope that there is a community of people out there who are willing to take a chance, who are willing to remove their chains for something different.

# Introduction: "Keep on Fishing"

It's a hot day. As I stare across the shoreline of Seabrook Island, South Carolina, all I can think is, "I hope I don't get a sunburn." When I burn, it's not pretty. Ask anyone in my family about it. They'll all tell you that when I burn, *everybody burns*. I quickly make my way over to my backpack, where I have a few extra bottles of sprayable sunscreen stored away. I proceed to shower myself in lotion when, suddenly, I hear a shout from behind me.

"Woah, John! Fish on."

It's my father. I drop the bottle and sprint toward the bending fishing rod. By the time I reach the pole, the rod is ready to snap. I grab ahold and yank. Whatever monstrosity is on the other end now has a hook firmly set in its jaw. Fish on. Hell, yeah! The fish is incredibly strong and fights hard. The reel is quickly letting out line, but that's okay; there's plenty more. I let the fish take as much as it wants. If I keep the line taut, the fish will eventually wear itself out.

My father walks over, cigar in hand. "What do you think it is?" He blows out a cloud of billowy smoke.

"I don't know, but it feels big."

My father quietly watches while I continue my dance with the fish. I can't help but imagine I am Santiago, fighting the massive Marlin that dragged him out to sea, in Ernest

Hemingway's classic, *The Old Man and The Sea*. Several moments go by and finally, the fish starts to succumb to its own exhaustive efforts. I begin the arduous task of reeling in the fish, making sure not to break the line in the process. As the fish gets closer to the shore, we get a brief glimpse at what it is. With sweat pouring down my face, muscles aching, and raw hands, I turn to my father with a huge smile on my face and say, "It's a shark."

I take several massive steps backward and pull the shark out of the water and up onto the shore. I get the shark into place where my father can grab it around the gills and straddle it. He does this to prevent the shark from thrashing around as he removes the hook from its mouth. As my father is relieving the shark of its superficial impalement, I am scrambling back to our gear to grab my phone in order to take some pictures. As I open my phone, I notice I have a few emails and app notifications waiting for me, but I ignore them. Instead, I swipe open my camera.

I proceed to snap a few pictures of the shark as the tidal waves softly lap around its shimmering, muscular body. It's a beautiful blacktip shark, around three to four feet in length.

My father asks, "Got enough pictures?"

"Yep. We're good."

My father drags the shark back to the water. As the water deepens and the swells become stronger, the shark begins to turn unruly. The shark strikes left then right, its head swinging around, attempting to mar its captor with its razor-sharp teeth. It wants to escape, to be free. *I can relate to that.* Finally, the shark is fully submerged and, in the blink of an eye, disappears amid a cloud of sand and salty foam. That's shark number three for the day and it's not even noon. We reset our bait and hurl the line back into the rolling waves.

My father relights his cigar, and I fetch us a couple of beers as a reward. On my way back to the cooler, I open my phone to check those pending notifications. One is a work order to add a blog article and brochure to the company website, and the other is a request to set up billing for a new account. I grab the beers and make my way back. I hand my dad his beer and set mine on the ground. I ask him if he could give me five minutes to handle a few things. He nods and says that he can handle the rods for a moment without me.

I jog to my backpack, pull out my Chromebook, fire up my hotspot, and quickly complete the tasks that were sent to me. I send a couple other emails to make sure everything else is running smoothly back at the office and then put everything away. I grab the sunscreen that I dropped earlier and walk back to the rods. I finish spraying myself, crack open my beer, readjust my sunglasses, and begin to watch for any sudden jerk of the rods.

The sun is shining and there's not a cloud in the sky. The water is warm, and the smell of salt is heavy in the air. The seagulls are cawing while hovering over our heads (trying to steal our bait, *bastards*). There's no one within half of a mile of us in either direction. We are quietly enjoying the moment and each other's company. Serenity.

It's just another ordinary Wednesday in the middle of June. As good a day as any to spend some time fishing on the beach. We should do this more often. *Why not*? Back home, the world is churning as it usually does. My father's company is making money and running smoothly, while the companies I work for are benefiting from the information and automation systems I set up a few months back. We are free to do what we want with our time.

# WORKING DIFFERENTLY: A PIRATE'S LIFE FOR ME

Living day to day, fidgeting in an uncomfortable chair, *tapping* hours of my life away into an Excel spreadsheet was the last thing I ever wanted to do. But, as I saw my life slowly turning toward that reality, I realized I had to find a way to escape. Much like the shark, my freedom was being taken away and I wasn't going to let that happen without a fight. As Jack Sparrow says in the movie, *Pirates of the Caribbean: On Stranger Tides*, "It's a pirate's life for me." The pirate's life, put another way, is a life built around *intentional* living. It is a lifestyle of freedom. It is a lifestyle dedicated to the principle of being able to do what you want when you want to do it. The pirate's lifestyle is living your dreams, having fun, and enjoying life today.

I once heard Tony Robbins, the world-famous performance coach and advisor to everyone from Bill Clinton to Mikhail Gorbachev, from Leonardo DiCaprio to Oprah, say, "[In life], we get what we tolerate." We get what we tolerate. Think about that. Everything you have in your life is there because you said, "Yes, I think this is good enough." You've settled. You've said that *this* person, *this* object, and *this* situation meets your minimum expectations. But, as you will find, minimum expectations are not good enough. Minimum expectation only gets you what's average or, as I like to call it, *normal.*

### LIFE IS ABOUT GROWTH

For me, working in an office, chained to a desk for eight hours a day for 40 years is the last thing that I ever want. Fuck that. Let me repeat myself: *fuck that*. Life is about growth. Growth comes from learning new things, experiencing new places, succeeding or failing with new challenges, and creating relationships with people from all walks of life. How in the hell can I (or anyone) grow while sitting behind a desk interacting with the same people, doing the same monotonous tasks for the rest of my life? I can't, and neither can you. If you aren't growing, you're dying. Unless you are ready to be buried in the ground or scattered into the ocean, it's time to free yourself from the confines of your office, regain control over your time, and start living for the now, rather than the later.

### THREE PILLARS OF HACKING NORMAL

To free yourself from the fetters of traditional office life, we will focus on three pillars. These three pillars have helped me up-end the traditional employee-employer relationship in a healthy and mutually beneficial way. You get autonomy; your boss gets value. With autonomy back in your hands, the *dream* of living life to the fullest becomes an immediate *reality* rather than a distant dream. The three pillars are: control over your *time*, *location*, and *income*.

# WHY WORK THE WAY WE DO?

When I started rethinking the way I worked, I wanted to know why society adheres to certain social norms in our current working environments. For instance, I wanted to know why everyone agrees to go into the office at 8 A.M. and to leave at 5 P.M. What was the logic behind those hours? Do people *really* work best during that time of day?

I also wanted to know why everyone sits in one place for most of the day, staring at a screen. Does being static make a person concentrate better? I wanted to know why people would stare out the window on beautiful days, instead of experiencing those days for themselves. Is it more fulfilling to dream about life than go out and live it? It doesn't make any sense. Lastly, why do we even need to go into an office? Does it really matter where we get our work done, as long as we get it done?

## ERUDITE ANSWER

We are a species that thrives on social comparison. From whom we date to where we work, we are constantly comparing to make sure that we are achieving something equal to or superior to our closest peers. Since we so heavily compare ourselves to each other, when we do something out of place, we feel awkward, weird, and out of touch. In fact, others put labels on us such as: *not a team player*, *socially awkward*, *strange*, and many more.

Perceiving someone or something to be out of place makes us feel like it doesn't belong. That's why we shun the weirdo in the cubicle down the hall or, if we look inward, stop being ourselves and take on the persona of the group or team we are a part of. In its purest form, we are experiencing what is commonly referred to as *groupthink*. Groupthink is dangerous because it stifles innovation and criticism. When you are perceived as going against the grain, there is a moment where those around you (and yourself) will feel uncomfortable.

## An Actual Answer

The more I questioned work, the more complicated and unexplainable it became. The best answer I could come up with was Tony Robbins' six basic human needs. These basic human needs can help us understand exactly why we work in the ways that we do. Take a moment to see how work has a solution for each basic human need. It's amazing.

### One: Certainty

Certainty is "our need to feel in control and to know what's coming next so we can feel secure." Certainty is the result of careful calculation in order to safeguard us from massive loss if we take the wrong step forward. It's the need to avoid pain and stress, but also to guarantee the most pleasure out of our current and future situations. As Tony says, "It affects how much risk we're willing to take in life – in our jobs, in our investments, and in our relationships." The greater our need for certainty, the less willing we will be to accept and emotionally stomach risk.

### Two: Uncertainty

Life also needs to push back occasionally. The failures and faults of life make the successes sweeter and more rewarding. Taking risks, both big and small, make life exciting.

There's a great *Twilight Zone* episode entitled *A Nice Place to Visit* that is a perfect anecdote to appreciate this idea. In the episode, a man named Rocky Valentine has died and gone to his own, personal heaven. In heaven, we see Rocky in a casino, surrounded by beautiful girls and winning every game he plays. He is unstoppable, has unlimited sway and persuasion over others. He is constantly fortunate and always gets what he wants. After a month of living in his personal heaven, Rocky starts to get *bored*. Since he always has his whims satisfied and always knows he is going to win at anything he attempts, Rocky starts to get angry. He demands that he lose at something just to add a little variety to his life, a little *uncertainty*. His frustration is best exemplified when he shouts, "If I gotta stay here another day, I'm gonna go nuts! I don't belong in Heaven, see? I want to go to the other place (hell)." Then, the guide who has been with him since the beginning of the episode (his name is Pip) says, "Heaven? Whatever gave you the idea that you were in heaven, Mr. Valentine? This *is* the other place!"

Even though we want everything to go our way, if it did, we would eventually grow bored and unsatisfied. Everyone, including you, needs some sort of uncertainty to put up with. As Tony Robbins says, "You can't grow muscle – or character – unless you have something to push back against." Don't seek security and safety, seek adventure. As Jim Rohn says, "It's better to live thirty years full of adventure than one hundred years safe in the corner."

### THREE: SIGNIFICANCE

Everyone needs to feel "significant" which means special, important, or unique. People get these feelings in a variety of ways. Some make lots of money. Some go after awards, championships, and other notable accomplishments. Some pursue advanced degrees and academic pedigree. Others dress flamboyantly - wearing unique hairstyles, tattoos or even body piercings. The underlying drive is finding a way to be unique and stand out from the crowd.

### FOUR: LOVE AND CONNECTION

Tony Robbins believes that, "Love is the oxygen of life; it's what we all want and need most." When we love at our utmost, we feel the full capacity of life. But losing love can hurt. Rather than risk the possibility of such loss, many people limit themselves to mere connections that lack the depth and intensity of deeper love. Still, connection is better than nothing. Connection can be found in friendship, prayer, appreciation of nature, and in other forms of intimacy. As Tony says, "If nothing else works, you can get a dog."

### FIVE: GROWTH

If you're not growing, you're dying. Tony echoes this sentiment repeatedly in everything that he does. Stagnation, complacency, and believing you know or have enough causes people to begin to wither away. I am a huge advocate of the idea that there is always something more you can do to grow. At different points in your life, what grows may change. You may reach a point where you make enough money to never worry about your bills, food, or extravagant vacations again. At that point, your financial growth may not need constant diligence anymore. But I would argue, this is when you pivot to something else. If finances are no longer a concern, then grow in intellect, spirituality, or connection. If those don't appeal, you can always grow in your capacity to give back.

### SIX: CONTRIBUTION

This world has given so much to you, even if you don't realize how much. Go be a teacher, consultant, volunteer, or, hell, a blood donor. Do something that integrates you into society in a giving way, not just a taking manner. There is always someone who would greatly appreciate the voluntary sacrifice of your time to help him build a shed or serve food in a soup kitchen. If you are willing to give of yourself, much comes in return. As Tony Robbins says, "Life's not about me; it's about we."

# Hacking Normal: Win Conditions

In the video game industry, there is a game design concept known as a "win condition." A win condition is the summation of actions and objectives that result in an individual winning a game. For example, in chess, the win condition is to get the opposing player's king into a situation where, no matter which direction the king moves, one of your pieces can take him down. Checkmate.

Work, like chess, is a game with certain win conditions. Thankfully, like chess, there are multiple ways to win (even if people don't know it). For work, our win condition is control over the three pillars. Those three pillars are:

1. Control over your *time.*
2. Control over your *location.*
3. Control over your *income.*

Now, like I said at the beginning, not every aspect of this book is going to be useful to everyone. This is true for the pillars as well. For this book to serve you, take what you like (what you can apply) and leave the rest. It is possible to hack work and win by achieving just one or two of these win conditions. If you can get all three, that's awesome. If you can't get all three right now, just achieve what you can and come back to the other ideas when your situation or skills have changed.

## WORK IS NOT A NEGATIVE

As you read through the following pages, I want to be very clear that I do not think work is bad or should be avoided. In fact, work is where we can look to understand our character, whether we can deliver value, and whether we can provide for a family. Work is *good*. But, like debt, work is a double-edged sword. How does that old trope about debt go? *Debt is a useful servant but a cruel master.*

I'd like to make the claim that work is a useful servant but a cruel master. If kept in check, with the use of the three pillars, work is an opportunity for each of us to become more than we are.

## SETTING GOALS

Goals are fascinating because they are the best way to define success for ourselves. Goals are how we hold ourselves accountable for the things that matter most to us. Without goals, it would be difficult for us to be motivated to complete most tasks. Goals, when created with a little enthusiasm and forethought, are a great way to figure out what we need to do with our lives.

But it all starts with a list. You must write your goals down. That makes them real. I have a journal where I keep several lists of goals. My lists include various areas of my life in which I would like to see myself accomplish goals in the coming months and years of my life.

Goals help us start with the end in mind. Without the end in mind, we are unable to define the steps needed to take effective action to reach our goals.

# S.H.M.A.T. Goals Versus S.M.A.R.T. Goals

In the beginning stages of my journey of hacking work, I did a lot of thinking about goal setting. I discovered something that kind of upset me in the process. I discovered that the traditional and ubiquitous idea of setting S.M.A.R.T. goals was wholly incompatible with what I needed to institute the three pillars. After a moment of frustration, I had a moment of brilliance (in my humble opinion) that completely changed the way in which I approach goals. It inspired me to come up with a new way to create goals. I call this new method: *S.H.M.A.T.*

For those of you who don't know, the S.M.A.R.T. method of setting goals stands for:

- *Specific*
- *Measurable*
- *Actionable*
- *Reasonable*
- *Timely*

On the surface, this is an extremely useful tool. It creates a system for setting goals that most people don't intuitively have. It's so effective that I spent years making goals based on this formula. With the S.M.A.R.T. method, I successfully attained some pretty awesome things.

But, like I said, I won't be using S.M.A.R.T. goals anymore. I'll be using S.H.M.A.T. S.H.M.A.T. stands for:

- *Specific*
- *Habitual*
- *Measurable*
- *Actionable*
- *Timely*

## WHAT'S THE DIFFERENCE BETWEEN S.M.A.R.T. AND S.H.M.A.T.?

The difference is subtle in the name, but major in implementation. S.M.A.R.T. goal setting means asking goals to be *reasonable*. Reasonable goals are goals that we know we can achieve; things that are within our reach. S.H.M.A.T., on the other hand, focuses on creating goals with *habitual systems* while, at the same time, not requiring you to stay within the realm of reason. S.H.M.A.T. goals only require that we do something on a regular basis, to move closer to achieving our goal.

## WHAT'S SO GROUNDBREAKING?

From the experience I have had making goals, I've always stuck within what I believed to be easily attainable – the reasonable. Yet, when I look at my life, I can honestly say that reasonable goals have given me nothing but fleeting moments of happiness. Their fault was that they were easy goals, like writing an article for my blog or keeping my phone on silent during dinner. They didn't ask *me* to become something *more*.

In other words, they were goals that didn't require anything more from me. They were easy. They were goals that made me feel like I was accomplishing something, but they just asked me to maybe be just a smidgen more disciplined. Because these goals never demanded me to become a different person, I never changed. I found myself taking only small steps forward, rather than major leaps.

S.M.A.R.T. goals kept me reasonable. S.H.M.A.T. goals helped me go against the grain.

If you start setting goals using the S.H.M.A.T. method, I implore you to start being unreasonable. Shoot for things that are significantly outside your reach. Those goals will demand that you implement both extra effort and discipline to achieve. Then, make it a daily habit to chip away at the obstacles preventing you from reaching those unreasonable goals.

### WHAT MAKES THE HABITUAL GOAL ANY DIFFERENT?

Unlike reasonable goals, habitual goals demand that you change something about yourself. They require you to realign your day, commit to practice, and have a long-tail view.

For example, let's say that I have the goal to become a millionaire. Some people might say that attaining a million dollars is unreasonable. Forget about that. Even if you never reach your goal, by building into your life the habit of working, acting, living, and visualizing yourself as a millionaire, you will find success. Even if that success only lands you at $850,000, you'll be much further ahead than those who set reasonable goals at $60,000.

The miraculous is not in the culmination and attainment of the goal (which is still sweet). The miraculous is in how the goal changes you. It's not the goal. It's who you become in pursuit of the goal.

## WHAT MAKES HABITUAL GOALS MORE POWERFUL THAN REASONABLE GOALS?

To me, habitual goals are always more effective because they are placed within the routine of our day. They aren't spin-offs or tangential distractions. They aren't half-baked dreams. Habitual goals become a foundational part of who we are – day in and day out.

Once something becomes a part of you, something crazy happens. You start seeing opportunities that could help you jump miles ahead toward your goal. It's the craziest, most hocus-pocus sounding thing in the world, but it's true.

If you are in the market to buy a Jeep Wrangler and you spend time each day looking for deals, figuring out the model and testing driving, suddenly, you'll start seeing Jeep Wranglers everywhere. It'll seem like everyone owns a Jeep.

It's obviously not true that everyone owns a Jeep, but what's happening is your mind is starting to highlight moments and opportunities where you can meet the thing you want. Your mind is trying to develop opportunities for you to attain your goal.

These almost ethereal moments can only come about if you've made it a daily habit to chip away at the obstacles impeding you from your goal.

### Try It Out

Make a S.H.M.A.T. goal. Pick anything that sounds interesting for you to attain. Don't worry about whether it is reasonable. Reasonable goals have always been the limiting factor in human (your) potential.

Try, instead, to set a crazy goal. Then, after you set that crazy goal, map out what daily activity you need to do in order to attain that goal. Then, with one step at a time, begin to chip away. One day, you'll find that you're closer to achieving your goal than you ever thought.

# THE PRIZE IS AUTONOMY

According to the Merriam-Webster dictionary, autonomy is defined as self-directing freedom and moral independence; the state of existing or acting separately from others.

If you are looking to escape the nine-to-five life, you need to be comfortable embracing the principles and responsibilities of autonomy. When you free yourself from the prison-like environment of your office, no one will be there to make sure that you are working at your computer, diligently typing away to finish your PowerPoints, uploading product images to the eCommerce portal, or finishing your CAD drawings by the end of business (EOB) on Friday. With autonomy comes the responsibility to provide yourself with self-motivation and direction. If you can't or aren't willing to take on that responsibility, *turn back now*.

This concept of autonomy, this freedom to make your own decisions, scares people. Like the allegory of the cave, when people are presented with the option to unfetter themselves from their desk and their cubicle, they freak out. They fear that they will resort to laziness and unproductive activities, like watching TV or scrolling through Facebook all day. To be completely honest, some people will fall into that reality. That is extremely disheartening. But, if you have a desire to work, to be a productive member of society, you will not let yourself sit in front of the TV while there is work to be done.

## SICK OF VACATION AND RETIREMENT

There are two other times in life that people experience this complete lack of responsibility. The first is *vacation*. Remember what those days feel like? At the beginning, you're glad to be rid of work and work's responsibilities. You want to sit by the pool, drink a margarita, and soak up the sun. But, by about the fifth day, your margarita starts to taste bland, your skin could use a break, and the chlorine is starting to do wild things to your hair. By the seventh day, most people are ready to go back to work. You didn't want a lifetime of vacation; you just wanted an hour (or so) a day to focus on you.

Speaking of a *lifetime* of vacation, this brings us to our second life experience, *retirement*. Ask people who are living in retirement how their life is after a year. Most of them are bored out of their minds. No worries, though: only another 20 years or more until they die.

## WHAT'S THE POINT?

People say they don't want to work, but that's bullshit. What people really want is to control how they work. They want autonomy to work on the things that matter and make them feel fulfilled and valuable. At the same time, they want to work in a way that doesn't put life on hold.

I'm of the opinion that autonomy means that I can work where, when, and how I want to. I prefer working outside the office in places like coffee shops, bookstores, or on the beach. These places make me feel centered and happy. Additionally, I prefer to get all my work done before noon so that I can plan meetings or activities in the afternoon. I once read that people should focus on the customer in the morning and administrative aspects in the afternoon. I've tried building my schedule around that, but your preferences may vary.

Autonomy doesn't mean that you must work outside of the office like I do. I have heard people say that they prefer working in an office because it gives them an incentive to work or an air of professionalism. To these people, I say, more power to you. Please, continue to go into the office if that's where you feel most productive. I don't want you to ever feel like you have to remove yourself from a place you feel productive, hence the win condition theory.

Take a moment to think about how many days you have spent sitting at your desk with nothing to do. If you are going to work in the office, ensure that you have the autonomy to decide whether sitting at a desk is a good use of your time. I don't want you to feel like you must sit at a desk and twiddle your thumbs until the clock strikes a certain hour. That is *unnecessary* torture. If you have real autonomy, you can work when there is work to do and have freedom to explore other activities, hobbies, or run errands when things are slow. If you had that kind of autonomy, how much better would working in an office be?

## AUTONOMY SEEKS EFFICACY

My modus operandi is to be as *efficient* and *effective* as possible to generate the greatest *efficacy*. The goal of any job is efficacy because efficacy is your time and effort focused on the *right* activities to generate the *greatest* results. For example, if you are a salesperson, wouldn't it be great to spend two hours [efficient] calling a highly qualified prospect list [effective] of people who want to buy [efficacy]? Of course! If you knew you could reach or surpass your sales goal by seeking out, implementing, and using efficacious processes, you'd do it. I would.

# PILLAR DEFINITIONS

## *TIME*

*Time* is the one resource that you can't get back. You only have so many seconds, minutes, hours, and days in your life. Find a way to make sure that you are using time how *you* want to use it. In a working environment, I want to control exactly *when* and *how long* I work.

*When* I work is very important to me. I don't know anyone who can say that they work best *only* during the hours between 9 a.m. and 5 p.m. There are times when I want to work at 5:30 in the morning or 10:30 in the evening.

*How long* I work dutifully follows suit with the idea of *when* I work. There is a mental trick that people play on themselves when they are in an office for eight hours a day. It's called Parkinson's Law. Essentially, Parkinson's Law states: a task will balloon in size in order to fit the time constraint given to the task. For example, give someone a week to get a PowerPoint presentation done and you will see the presentation on your desk at the close of business on Friday. That's just how humans act.

I hate working within the constraints of Parkinson's Law. I'm all about getting the task done now. But that is only true if, when the task is done, I can be free to focus on or do something else. I want to be paid for efficient use of my time, not how well I can waste it. If I don't have something to work on, I'm not at my desk or at the office.

## LOCATION

Speaking of not being at the office, this brings us to my second area of control: *location*. I *will not* spend my days in an office. Period. Unless I must be in the building for a meeting or important task, I work elsewhere. There is no reason to be in an office for eight hours a day. I am most productive when I can work in an environment that stirs my creativity. Sometimes, that means I am working next to a waterfall or by the ocean. Most of the time, though, it means working quietly at my home office at 6:00 a.m. while listening to a podcast or soothing music.

Having control over my location has many benefits, such as saving myself from traffic, getting to exercise when my body is ready, to live where I want to live, and, if I had kids, to spend time with them when they aren't at school. All the things that people feel like they are missing (and are missing), I get to experience daily.

## INCOME STREAMS

My financial goal is to have multiple income streams; somewhere around seven would be optimal. Those income streams can come from anywhere: jobs, investments, my own company, book sales, etc. The point, though, is that I am not dependent on one company or one source to meet all my financial needs. As an employee, I want to work for two or three companies at a time to provide an income buffer. To most people, that sounds like a lot. But if you have control over your time and location, having three jobs is not that bad. You work for each company when each company needs you to work; no more, no less.

If a company has a problem with me spreading my time and focus over multiple sources, then, well, it's not going to work out. The beauty of multiple income streams is two-fold. First, I have all the leverage. I no longer must take a crappy employment deal because I am desperate for money. If I'm just adding another company to the list of companies I am already working for, the company has no power over me. I can accept or reject their employment offer at will. That is an amazing power most people never get to experience. Second, I have protection. Let's say that a company thinks I am underperforming and decides to fire me. If my only source of income was from that company, I'd be up shit creek. But, since I have multiple sources of income, I can be fired (or I can quit) from a job and still retain a source (or multiple sources) of income, due to my work with the other companies. Simply put, it's not a disaster if I get let go or quit my job.

# A GLIMPSE OF THE FUTURE

Richard Branson once said, "In this increasingly connected world, you really can work from anywhere." If you read between the lines, hidden within this statement is a complex world that few of us have taken the time to truly appreciate and prepare for. Richard Branson, though he may not know it, is talking about the future of work. The traditional notions of what it means to work for yourself or for a company are about to be turned on their heads. It's inevitable. The only question is, can you see and adapt to the changes before you are left behind?

The idea of being able to work anywhere in the world is not a new one. People have been working and contributing to international companies, products, and efforts for decades. But, with the advent of the Internet and cloud computing, it should be no surprise to you: distance and location matter less than they ever have in history. If the work gets done and the product or service is delivered, does it matter where the work happens? No.

Despite what others might think or what you might believe, remote work is on the rise and is going to become the new normal. Companies are using outsourced, remote workers more than ever because they are cheaper, specialized, and can work while the rest of the company sleeps. Remote work is no longer just a gig for the newly graduated student while they search for a more stable job. No, remote work is a career choice for individuals who are willing to take on the responsibilities and high standards of an autonomous life. Remote work is not only providing lucrative cash flows for people, but also extreme personal freedom.

## HALLMARKS OF THE FUTURE

According to an article in Fast Company magazine, future workers are going to be drawn to remote work because it offers various lifestyle opportunities that young professionals and some seasoned professionals value more than a paycheck.

### *LOCATION INDEPENDENCE*

Young professionals are looking to control where they live. Some want to live in the mountains of Colorado, others in the rolling plains of Montana, and some in the hustle and bustle of New York City. Location independence offers workers the ability to work for the company of their choosing (one that reflects their values and skills) while, at the same time, living in places that reflect their personality and intrinsic values. No longer will employees be forced to work only for companies that are local. The door is wide open to work for anyone, anywhere.

### *REAL-LIFE IS ACCESSIBLE AGAIN*

As we move away from working conditions and the ideals of the Industrial Revolution (yes, most of the standards for work today are that archaic), people are taking better care of themselves, their relationships with people, and their communities. Health and social consciousness are becoming major concerns for people. On top of that, people want the freedom to care for sick or troubled loved ones without fearing the wrath of an employer for not being in the office. The finer things in life are no longer the brand-new BMW, but moments like watching a baby take her first steps or watching the leaves fall as the seasons change. Intrinsic value is beginning to trump extrinsic materialism. The relationship between work and life needs to reflect those changes.

## Focus on Efficacy

Buzzwords that used to make companies excited such as *efficiency* and *effectiveness* are losing their impact. Most employees and employers don't want to work toward shaving two seconds off their production time anymore. Instead, they want to work on making sure that each action is going to bring about the greatest return on investment. In other words, companies and employees want to focus on things that bring about efficacious results. *Efficacy* is all about doing the things that bring about exponential change. When people know they are working on things that are going to have an immense impact on the company and the customers, they work harder and care more about their work.

## Increased Engagement

Employees, especially the younger generations, are going to want to work when they are at their best. The typical nine-to-five workday simply doesn't *work* for everyone. Some people, like myself, prefer to work at different hours of the day, when we are more focused. When an employee is more focused, performance is better, and tasks get done more quickly and accurately.

## Time Flexibility

When a company is flexible and allows its employees to own their work schedules, they are empowering the employees to become their best. Companies also turn themselves into a cohesive, 24-hour machine. As employees are spread out over different time zones and operating at different optimal times of the day, work is constantly moving forward.

## Statistics Worth Mentioning

According to a survey run by FlexJobs.com, a major online employment network for remote workers, 65 percent of workers think they would be more productive telecommuting versus working in a traditional workplace. That's phenomenal. When asked to elaborate, employees say that working from home makes them more productive because they can better juggle their work and life responsibilities.

Some workers want to be able to pack a lunch for their kids in the morning as they see them safely to the bus, while others want to get to the gym before they start their day. Personally, I like taking 20 minutes before my workday to read, meditate, or practice a new language via an app like Duolingo. In the same survey, when asked, "Where do you go when you have a really important work task or project to do?" 93 percent of people said it isn't the office. According to the FlexJobs survey, only 7 percent of workers say the office is their location of choice if they need to be most productive on important work-related projects. What about you?

## Just a Fad?

What if this "remote work thing" is just a fad? That's a legitimate concern, but according to research performed by Elite Daily, 60 percent of office jobs will be remote by 2022. At the time of writing this, that's less than five years away. If you believe that you're protected by being in the 40 percent that won't or can't become remote, Elite Daily also discovered that, within the next 25 years, the "normal" working hours will be erased. Working days will change to just a few hours of tasks a day *or week*. What are you going to do with all that extra time when your workday ends before noon? These are real questions and predicaments that you must start thinking about.

As a side note, if you think your job is protected because you work in a S.T.E.M. (*S*cience, *T*echnology, *E*ngineering, and *M*athematics) field, it's not. Companies want the best scientists, mathematicians, designers, and engineers (structural, software, hardware, etc.) in the world. With countries like India and China quickly catching up to and, frankly, surpassing the U.S. in the areas of S.T.E.M., companies are investing in infrastructure and cloud technology that allows for outsourced individuals to work and deliver their products instantly over the Internet. In other words, you're no longer competing with the local guy, you're now competing with everyone in the world who wants to do the job.

## Don't Freak Out

I don't want to freak you out with doom and gloom. The world isn't ending, and jobs are not going to completely disappear due to automation like many think they will. But I do want you to grasp the impending change that is coming. Don't worry, though, I'm not in the business of scare tactics and fear mongering. I'm not trying to get rich off fear or drama. I'm a genuinely positive guy, and I want you to succeed. So, let's look at the positives that are coming down the pipeline.

First, I want you to realize that even though companies have every capability and right to outsource their entire operation overseas, they won't. There's something about a native that is familiar and trustworthy. Take advantage of that.

Second, you've got an amazing opportunity to own this new job reality. As someone reading this book, you are getting in before the storm. Remember, 2022 is the published milestone for when companies will start making major changes and transitioning to remote workers. This is the time to act and make yourself, as Cal Newport says, "So good, they can't ignore you." We will learn about Cal and his idea about being unignorable later. For now, know that to survive in this remote future, *skills* will trump passion every time. In fact, if you approach this new work economy with the idea that you'll be able to work only on things that you are passionate about, you'll have a hard time surpassing others and retaining your streams of income. We'll talk about multiple sources of income later, as well.

Third, this new work economy might make it seem like a lot of your previous knowledge will be useless, but that is far from the truth. The skills of marketing, engineering, or teaching aren't going away – the only thing that is changing is the medium through which the work is performed. Opportunity is not disappearing – in fact, opportunity is becoming more abundant. With this new work economy, it is possible for you to carve out your own niche of expertise, in which you can provide your services, experience, or knowledge in industries that have a high demand for your skills. The only caveat: you need to become the best that you can be. Bring value to the marketplace and constantly watch for the latest practices, trends, and tools to help you do more. In order to succeed, you'll need to implement a system for constantly learning and improving.

# PASSION IS BULLSHIT

Starting in the 1970s, an entire industry has been built around the idea of finding and pursuing your passion (or purpose). I'm certain you have brushed up against the products and tools of this industry multiple times in your life. Those tools include self-help books, personality tests, seminars, and online support groups. There is a wide variety of places online where people go to get help finding their passion.

The forums, tests, groups, books, and seminars *do* have a beneficial goal: *to help people live or work in a way that fills the individual with pride and meaning.* They want to help people discover their *passion*. It's an admirable mission. The problem is passion doesn't come before action. No one woke up one day and said, "My passion is pumping human excrement (a.k.a., shit) out of homes, port-o-potties, and septic tanks. I think I'll get a job doing that. Maybe I'll even start my own business!?" In reality, someone realized that the market needed a company to remove human waste from homes, outhouses, and other areas of disposal, built a company, learned the ins and outs of doing their job well, and then began to innovate and improve the process. The passion for their job came way down the line, possibly years after they removed their first tankful of last night's Tex-Mex chili.

The septic tank removal service isn't the only example out there. If you ever saw the show *Dirty Jobs*, hosted by Mike Rowe, you got to see all sorts of weird jobs people do to fill a hole in the market. Some of those people were *good* at what they did and expressed passion about their jobs, but it is safe to say that they didn't start off passionate; they had to grow into their passion.

I remember, in both college and high school, being given personality assessments to help me understand who I was, so that I could find my passion. If you took one of those tests, you'll remember that you were supposed to take the results and use them to study the right subjects, work for the right company, and get to feel happy. The problem is, no matter how much I tried to align myself to those perfect ideals, I never seemed to find happiness or fulfillment in my work. The magical moment where the heavens open and choirs of angels usher me to my desk has never occurred. And why not? Because passion is bullshit.

Cal Newport wrote a great book about passion called *So Good They Can't Ignore You*. I highly recommend you pick up his book. It's an easy read and goes into detail about the history of passion and how it is ultimately damaging to someone entering the job market. Now, I don't want to steal Cal's thunder, but I need to summarize a bit of his book to keep us moving forward.

Cal's book starts off by defining the generally accepted way of pursuing work for Baby Boomers and Millennials. He labels his definition the *passion hypothesis*. The passion hypothesis states, "The key to occupational happiness is to first figure out what you're passionate about and then find a job that matches that passion." That sounds exactly like what every counselor (who all obviously hated their jobs, by the way) and well-meaning person has told me my entire life. Since so many people were chanting the same mantra, I took it to heart when picking a college, my major(s), my summer jobs, and what I did in my free time. In the end, it was terrible advice.

## A Trip Down Memory Lane

Think back on who you were in high school or your early years of college. What were your passions back then? If I think back on who I was in high school, I shudder with shame. If I had pursued the things I was passionate about during those years, I'd be the laziest, most useless human being in the world. What about you? Who would you have been? It's amazing to me that we ask people who know almost nothing about themselves to make major financial and life decisions, based on this false concept of passion. To further drive the point home, I usually *lied* about my passions. I would make them up on the spot to appease the person asking. Simply put, depending on who asked me and what the situation was, I would give completely different answers because they were the right answers at the time. I guess it's safe to say that *pathological lying* was one of my many passions as a young adult.

I spent years of my life and tens of thousands of dollars pursuing a passion that a 17-year-old thought was going to be important. And what did a 17-year-old me think was important? For starters, I was good at playing *Guitar Hero* on expert mode, which obviously has great skill transfer into the job market [heavy sarcasm]. I don't think I need to say more. Now, do some 17-year-olds have their shit together? Of course. I, on the other hand, did not. The advice to follow my passion was a major mistake.

## THREE REASONS WHY YOU SHOULDN'T PURSUE PASSION

First, according to Cal, *passion that transitions into a career is extremely rare.* There are examples where the people excelling in their situation found their passion when they were young. The most common examples can be found in the world of professional athletes. You'd be hard pressed to find a professional athlete who says, "Oh, football, pssh, I picked it up last summer. And, wouldn't you know it, I just happened to be better than everyone else who started playing the sports when they were seven. Before that, I thought my calling was accounting."

It's important to note that just because there *is* an example of passion preceding profession doesn't disprove the "passion is bullshit" theory. In fact, both Cal and I agree that it strengthens the theory. Ask any scientist and they will tell you that in most studies, there are anomalies that occur outside of the statistical bounds of the experiment. Those anomalies do not override the average results of the entire experiment. They are considered, but not deemed, the likely result if someone were to duplicate the experiment. When we take a 10,000-foot view of the entire landscape, the average shows us that professional athletes are extremely rare when compared to the total number of people who ever played a sport. A similar comparison would be the number of lottery winners versus lottery players. Just because *someone* wins doesn't mean *you* suddenly become more likely to win. The reality is, in terms of statistics, it is highly unlikely that you will ever win, no matter how often you play.

Second, *to become passionate about something takes time.* Passion is not the precursor to a successful endeavor. Passion, instead, comes from *successfully experimenting* and then attaining the skills and habits necessary to achieve practiced competence. Passion is the result of learning, applying, failing, reassessing, learning, failing some more, finally succeeding, and then replicating the model. The driving force of passion is a daily, habitual exercise of competencies.

To prove this, let's look back at the guy or girl who removes human excrement from various places of ill repute. No one in their right mind wakes up excited about shoveling shit, yet I've had a guy come by the house and clean out a septic tank with a big smile on his face and a jovial, joking attitude. The guy loved what he was doing. When this person got to the job site, it wasn't shoveling shit that excited him. It was doing a job quickly, efficiently, and effectively that made him happy. When asked how he got into the business of cleaning out septic tanks, he said, "It was a way to pay bills." When asked why he stayed, he said, "Because I'm good at it." With further conversation, it was revealed that he had been cleaning out septic tanks for around seven years. He had seen every type of situation imaginable and nothing about a septic tank scared him. And *that* leads us to our last point.

Third, *passion is a side effect of mastery.* Have you ever heard an industry leader give a speech about the future of his or her company or the future of his or her craft? The fire that such individuals speak with is truly mesmerizing. That fervor only comes once someone has reached a level of mastery. Then, and only then, am I willing to say that a person is driven by passion. When you have seen and experienced every up and down in your industry or job, when there's no more uncertainty, when there's no more fear, and there's nothing left but possibility, that's where passion comes in.

When we look at passion as a side effect of mastery, it's easy to see why the guy who has pumped septic tanks for seven years loves his job. He doesn't love his job because every day is easy or cozy. I'm sure there are plenty of days where the problems are exhausting, and the weather is unbearable. He loves his job because, at the end of the day, he knows he can overcome any obstacle. With every obstacle he overcomes, he becomes even more valuable.

# CONTROLLING: TIME

*Time* is the one truly scarce and limited resource that we cannot get back. You only have so many seconds, minutes, hours, and days; you might as well make sure that you are using them in the best way(s) possible. Because time is a nonrenewable resource, it is the most valuable commodity we possess. Yet, for some reason, we willingly throw it away by remaining in dead-end jobs that bring us neither feelings of personal achievement nor opportunities to experience life to the fullest. Instead, we waste away, tethered to the idea that we are sacrificing our time now for greater time in the future.

This, unfortunately, is a fallacy. The future is not guaranteed to anyone; therefore, you cannot invest your time into the future. A man named Steve Bates, a small businessman in the Cincinnati area, opened my eyes to this reality of life when he said, "A majority of elderly people that I know, have said that the final ten years of their life [during retirement] have been underwhelming and unfulfilling." Steve explained to me that these people *waited* for their dreams to come to them, rather than seeking them out. They saw retirement as the moment when their dreams would come to fruition. Finally, when retirement did come, they found themselves unable to live a life like they had dreamed they would. Steve explained that lots of factors kept them from achieving the high level of fulfillment they desired. The causes are too many to list, but common causes were: health problems, financial instability, lack of motivation, and fatigue. The point is, these people waited their entire lives to do something exciting, and when it came time to pull the trigger, they couldn't. The dream had slipped away.

## MONEY VALUE OF TIME (MVT)

There's a fundamental concept in finance called the *time value of money* (TVM). The time value of money says: money available now is worth more than *the same amount in the future* due to its potential earning capacity over time. To possibly oversimplify the concept, $10 today is *likely* going to be worth more *now* than $10 in thirty years due to factors such as inflation and taxes. Money, therefore, loses value, unless it is invested into something that can grow faster than the factors trying to subtract value.

The time value of money also assumes that our money will continue to have value indefinitely. Sure, the spending power of a dollar may rise and fall over time, but the *concept* of money (the ability to hold and transfer value) will always exist. There will always be a demand for some means of transferring value, whether in paper bills, digital code, or animal furs. Thus, *money has longevity* and the ability to transfer value into new systems as they evolve.

Here's where the problem comes in: *you* do not have the same growth and longevity capacity as money. Money will outlast your knees, your back, your mental facilities, and your desires. Money doesn't have an expiration date – you do. You, an organic ball of matter, will degrade and lose capacity and value in the marketplace. You, a mere mortal, must succumb to the inevitability that your time will run out. Yet, many of us treat our finite amount of time as if we can invest it in a "time portfolio" that will compound and grow. Because of this, we are okay with telling ourselves that we can spend 40 hours a week sitting at a desk instead of playing with our kids or riding a bike through the fall leaves as winter approaches.

We somehow believe that by spending 30 years sitting behind a desk and sacrificing our time to the gods of industry, we will get paid in scores when we reach our retirement. Sorry, but that's bullshit. That's not how time works for humans. Treating yourself like a stock portfolio that will grow by 8 percent annually is nonsensical and leads to an unhappy and unfulfilled life.

When it comes to spending or investing our scarce resource of time, we believe in a fallacy that states: sacrificing our time *now* will give us *more* and *better* time in the *future*. That's the dream that most Baby Boomers and their progeny ascribe to, but it's wrong. Bronnie Ware wrote a book called *The Top Five Regrets of the Dying*, where she cultivated and shared her census of the regrets people have while on their deathbeds. What were the top two regrets on the list? First, *I wish I had lived a life true to myself, not what others expected of me.* Second, *I wish I hadn't worked so hard.*

Ding. Ding. Wake up! The top two regrets of the dying are that they didn't spend more time living life how they wanted to (rather than living the way society told them to live) and that they worked so hard (sacrificing all their time to the company). Yet, even with this unbelievably eye-opening book, we insist on forcing people down a *normal* path that so many regret when it comes to the end.

## Changing the Value Proposition

With that in mind, I want to propose the idea that we should begin to operate within a system built on the principle I call *money value of time* (MVT). The *money value of time* says that the *time* available *now* is worth more than the same amount in the future, due to the future's potential to simply not exist because of unforeseeable and unpredictable variables. This core principle of *life* holds that any amount of *time* is worth more now than it is later.

The money value of time assumes that our time is finite. Until someone can cheat death and live indefinitely, the only time that is guaranteed to us is the time we have experienced or are currently experiencing. There is no promise of tomorrow. Therefore, *time is limited* and highly valuable.

Time is most valuable in the current moment. Time, unlike money, cannot be protected by investing it in another source. The loss of time is permanent. When used unwisely and without a desire for efficacy, the loss of time is compounded. The loss is compounded because if time could have been better used doing another task or used for a greater experience, you leave less time for another experience or moment. *Time cannot be invested and cannot compound to yield an 8 percent increase annually.*

The money value of time concept has helped me to see the importance of today, instead of dreaming about what could happen tomorrow. This means that your time in the *present moment* is worth more than the same amount of time in the future. Sacrificing your time today for some future gain is a divestment, not an investment. If this idea is groundbreaking, good, but it shouldn't be. All of us apply this idea of the *money value of time*, we just don't realize it.

The MVT is a rational decision that all of us make when we want to weigh the cost and benefit of action we are about to take. It's what Greg McKeown, author of *Essentialism*, calls *trade-offs*. Trade-offs decide the value of your time. What you decide to do now instead of something else is an evaluation of something's worth when compared to your time. MVT is why you chose to mow the lawn yesterday, not today. MVT is why you chose to hit the snooze button twice this morning. MVT is the reason why you chose to listen to your friend's advice concerning political issues instead of investigating the issues on your own. Ultimately, MVT boils down to what matters most *now*. When you apply this to work, you'll be surprised how your priorities change.

For example, you could choose to spend your time working eight hours a day, Monday to Friday at the office, making $35,000 per year while daydreaming about kayaking down a river over the weekend. With that reality, you would be just like everyone else in society. You would be investing all your optimal time during the week, hoping for a fun-fueled release for 48 hours over the weekend.

*Or...*

You could work the same job (or a different job) at $35,000 per year, but only spend three hours a day getting your tasks done and the last five hours of your work day kayaking on the river, while listening to an entire Beethoven symphony or reading your favorite book.

Here's my big question to you: *if you could complete your daily tasks in three hours and then have the rest of the day to do whatever you wanted with your time, do you think you could?* If you said yes, why isn't that what's happening now?

## Paying Attention to the Basics

In the book *Essentialism*, by Greg McKeown, Greg presents the idea of figuring out what is most important in our individual lives. To Greg, essentialism is giving yourself, "...permission to stop trying to do it all, to stop saying yes to everyone. Essentialism is making the highest contribution to the things that really matter."

Essentialism, in other words, is a focus on the things that matter most in your life. Now, what matters most is going to vary. There is no objective truth about what should matter in everyone's life. For me, I need to know that my basic finances are covered, that I can spend time with family and close friends, that I can keep myself in shape, and that I can develop my understanding of the world through reading and experiencing new things. These are the areas of my life that mean the most to me. In order to achieve those priorities in a healthy way, I need to make sure that I am pursuing the essential.

After you have taken some time to really understand what is most important in your life, it's time to ask yourself, are you investing in the right activities to ensure that you get the most out of life? Jim Rohn said, "Life is not measured by the seconds on the clock, but, instead, by our experiences – their frequency and intensity." And that's important to understand. Life is about *experiences*. No one in their right mind wants to hear about how you answered 50 emails in one day, but they would love to hear about how you summited the fourth tallest mountain in the world. One is an experience; one is busy work. One is essential; one is not.

And that's the point I want to make in this section about *trade-offs*. We can choose one of two paths in life: we can spend our days absorbed in busy work that has no real impact on our development, *or* we can spend our days doing the things that have meaning. Do we live by design or do we live by default? Understanding and evaluating these things is called deciding between *trade-offs*. *Trade-offs* will help you uncover a life that focuses on what matters most. Many of us major in minor things. We find ways to make mountains out of molehills and allow the trivial bullshit to overcome and devalue the things that matter most. What's worse is that we build our schedules (our time) around giving more attention to the things that do not matter. To quote Greg, "If you don't prioritize your life, someone (or something) else will."

Unfortunately, that's what work has done for most of us. Work has become that *something* that prioritizes our lives. Don't feel bad, though. Work, in its purest form, *is good*. It is only when work is no longer under your control that it turns into a cruel master.

## WHAT IS A TRADE-OFF?

*"Strategy is about making choices, trade-offs. It's about deliberately choosing to be different."* – Michael Porter

Trade-offs are the first step in regaining control of our time. They allow us to choose how our precious minutes are spent, rather than someone or something else choosing for us. Trade-offs are the calculated consequences that we decide to accept or deny when we make a choice. For instance, the fact that you are reading this book is a choice that has consequences.

You have either chosen to accept the consequences or you are blind to them. And, because you have made this choice, you are putting off other things that you could be doing such as watching TV, going for a run, or planning for a presentation you have next week. At the core of this choice is the *trade-off*. You have calculated, either consciously or unconsciously, that reading this book is a better use of your time and efforts than doing *literally* anything else (by the way, I'm honored).

## THE HARD PART ABOUT TRADE-OFFS

The hard part about understanding and using trade-offs is knowing which actions are best. I mean, that's the goal, right? Wouldn't you want every choice you make to deliver the highest return? Of course. But, if you are not in the practice of evaluating the trade-offs of life, it is very easy for some things to completely derail you from those that matter.

### STARTING SMALL

Here's how I started evaluating things in order to get the most efficacious results. I started small. I started with a few easy, daily disciplines that I knew were going to be beneficial to me in the long run. Every morning, I woke up and immediately got into the shower rather than hit the snooze button. I found that I had more energy throughout the day when I got up immediately, rather than wasting another nine minutes in a restless sleep. Then I tried eating a healthy breakfast and, while I ate, instead of reading Facebook or the terrors of life from random news sites, I put on either soft classical music and meditated or I listened to excerpts of personal development from gurus such as Jim Rohn and Tony Robbins. I chose to fill my head with calm, positive thoughts in the morning, rather than the drama of social media or the chaos of life. I found that this kept me vibrant and jovial throughout the day rather than pessimistic and gossipy.

## GOING BIGGER

Then, once I started mastering the small stuff, I decided to take on bigger things. Now, *bigger* doesn't mean I was upending my entire schedule for something completely different. Instead, I started to carve chunks of time out of my day to focus on things that I knew were going to benefit me in the long run. I started taking 30 minutes of my lunch to read books in order to learn something new about myself (or my work industry). I began to write small blog posts for my website to help me cement the ideas from those books in my head. That meant that I was more likely to use them in my daily life.

## GOING MAJOR

Only when I had established healthy routines and a constant appetite for learning and bettering myself did I start to change major parts of my life. I began to weigh the trade-offs I was making financially, emotionally, and physically. At first, it was painful. I didn't want to come to grips with the fact that watching Netflix before going to bed was screwing up my sleep schedule (which was the cause of some irritableness that I couldn't shake). I didn't want to succumb to the idea that I didn't need to spend nine hours of my day working when four hours would suffice (I felt like I was a piece of shit for not working the whole day like everyone else). But, like getting up and *not* hitting the snooze button, evaluating the trade-offs of these changes was going to put me in a place that I wanted to be in 5 or 10 years. And *that* was exciting.

## SHORT TERM VERSUS LONG TERM

When I first started evaluating trade-offs, I didn't know which actions were going to be good and which were going to be bad. The reality is, no one does. We must decide and reflect on the consequences. If it was a choice between something clearly bad versus something clearly good, it would only take us a millisecond to choose one path over the other. But, when we evaluate our actions based on two outcomes that we would like, it's a challenge.

I would venture to say that it's even more challenging when we must weigh two options that are *beneficial* to us. Often, one is an immediate benefit while the other is a longer-term benefit. For instance, investing in a Roth IRA is a great idea in the long run. It's such a good idea that I believe everyone should max theirs out every single year.

But, in the short run, it sucks having to give up over $5,000 of disposable income. Buying a new car, purchasing new clothes, and going out to eat with friends is undoubtedly more exciting than investing in a Roth IRA, but those short-term gains are nothing compared to the compounded benefit you'll get by investing in a Roth IRA over 40 years.

As someone who is looking to change his or her life, you need to be able to make the tough choices. Sometimes, though, those tough choices aren't going to pan out in your favor. Hence, why I started small. When you start small, you give yourself the opportunity to exercise your trade-off muscle.

As you recognize which trade-offs are better than others, start adding more "weight" to your choices. For a while, this new weight might be difficult, but as you exercise your trade-off muscle more, you'll find that even these new choices will get easier and easier to make. I always like to ask myself the following questions: *Who am I becoming? Will option A or will option B be the most direct path to the life I want to live?*

## TASK RECYCLING

What good are trade-offs if we don't have a systematic process to help us evaluate them? Not very good at all. Thus, we move to the next topic that is key to helping us make the best use of our time, task management. There are multiple ways in which we can begin to make better choices about the tasks that confront us each day. One of my favorite techniques of all is *task-recycling.*

Task-recycling is accomplished through a series of five steps.

Step 1. Delete
Step 2. Automate
Step 3. Hand Off
Step 4. Recycle (...and return Task to Step 1)
Step 5. Tackle

What I love about task-recycling is that it gives you permission, as well as a process, to take a step back from any choice that is laid out in front of you. I am a firm believer that choices need to be evaluated in the right light with the appropriate amount of time. If anyone tries to force you to decide without first weighing the consequences of what your decision could mean, they are trying to scam you. Let's break down the steps to see how they can help.

## STEP 1. DELETE

The French writer Antoine de Saint-Exupéry said, "Perfection is achieved not when there is nothing more to add, but when there is nothing left to take away." Simply addition by subtraction. The perfect house is clean, tidy, and clutter-less. So, why do we have a different line of thinking when it comes to work? It seems to me that many people try to fill their day with bullshit that doesn't help them do their jobs.

As assignments and inquiries cross our desks, we need to begin to evaluate them through the first lens of the task-recycling process: *Delete*. Deleting certain tasks is by far the most effective way to multiply your time. These are things that, if we stopped doing, would cause no disruption in the flow of the workday. One of my favorite deletion practices is to never answer the phone.

Many of the tasks that come across your desk are trivial. Yet, many of us do them because they seem like good business practices. Here are a few examples:

1. *Reconsidering a decision*: Also known as second-guessing yourself or getting someone else's opinion. Not only are you wasting your time, but you are wasting someone else's time in order to affirm a decision you have made. Be confident in your choice and move forward. There is no need to stop and reevaluate, unless new information comes to the forefront. Eliminating this saved me around two hours a week.

2. *Needless meetings*: Are you having meetings because *"it's what we do on Thursday"* or because there is a real

reason to bring everyone together? If it is a real reason, good, have the meeting. Make sure there is an agenda, a team leader, and a specific end time to ensure that the meeting doesn't stray off course. If you are having the meeting because you've always had the meeting, get rid of it. Doing this alone saved me around four hours a week.

3. *Emails*: By far the best way to reach me is by email, but email is also my pet peeve. Many people use email to relay *way* too much information. An email, in my opinion, never needs to scroll and should be written in the form of bullet points. Now, if the email is going out as a newsletter and needs to be more professional, fine, write a long email. But, when it comes to communication with the team members, email should be short and sweet. Also, I make it my mission to only check email three times a day: once when I start my workday, once after lunch, and once before I cease to be reachable until tomorrow. All other times of the day are meant for intensive work, not email anticipation and response. Putting a stop to constantly checking my email saved me around two hours a week.

4. *Doing someone else's job*: I'll admit it, I'm sort of a dick about this. This comes in two parts: first, you are doing another person's work and, second, other people are getting into your work. Let's tackle the first one: *don't do someone else's job*. Why? Because, despite what you might think and feel, you're not being a good Samaritan. You're enabling bad time and project management skills. As much as it sucks, sometimes you must let people sink.

This does two things for the person: One, it teaches them to stay on top of their tasks and ask for help when they are confused - rather than when they are drowning, and two, it shows the manager of that person how much work the employee can or cannot handle. Just like you shouldn't do another person's job, *don't let other people do your job*. Have you ever heard the phrase, *too many cooks in the kitchen*? If so, you probably understand that it means that when too many people give their input on a subject (a recipe for cooks), the result tends to be inferior. If you've been hired for a job, do the job, then ask for feedback. Don't let others intrude or give you feedback while you are working, unless you specifically ask for it.

## START WITH "NO"

The first step to begin eliminating things from your work docket is to start saying *no*. I'll admit, I went a little crazy with this initially. I was saying no to everything. It felt good. Eventually, though, I was able to calculate the trade-offs of what saying *yes* to this and *no* to that would be. I first had to establish a hard boundary. Others had to realize that not every request they presented was going to get my attention. I was especially strict on things that were deemed as "emergencies." In my opinion, nothing is an emergency. What the person is really saying when they are claiming an emergency is, "Help! I didn't plan my time or tasks appropriately. Save me!" An emergency is just a way for someone to ask you to do his or her work (and we are eliminating that from our diet).

I have a distinct memory of a coworker melting down during a phone call (this was before I stopped taking calls) about how a sales representative needed a video shot, edited, rendered, and delivered to her booth at a conference *in Germany* for a product that was shipping out of our warehouse by the end of the business day to a customer in Alabama. In her words, this was an *emergency* and we needed to act *now*. Mind you, it was 2:30 P.M. when I got this call, and I worked remotely (which we will talk about in the section about controlling your location). To produce this video was, to put it lightly, impossible in the timeframe we had available. The time it would take to take the product off the truck, set up the machine, operate, shoot (including editing, voiceovers, and final rendering), and reload (back onto the truck), far exceeded the two and a half hours we had available to us.

Instead of stressing myself out and rushing over to miss the deadline and put even more people behind, I evaluated the trade-offs and chose to say no to my frantic coworker.

I suggested that we pull an image from our database of machines in a laboratory setting to be sent to the people in Germany. From Germany, they could get it blown up and printed for the conference floor. I created an online form for the salespeople that could capture the contact information of interested prospects that integrated with our marketing automation and CRM systems. I told the sales people to inform any prospect that a video was being created to fully explain the ins and outs of the machine, but, since it was such a "new" product of ours, we were a little behind on our promotional material (putting the blame on me). Everyone calmed down. The "emergency" was solved because I practiced the art of saying *no*.

## STEP 2. AUTOMATE

*"If it's not a process, it's a problem." –* Scott Adams, *The Dilbert Principle*

Whenever I get the opportunity to corner someone and talk about my new, hacked way of working, I get a little overzealous when the topic of automation comes up. I love the idea that everything can be systematized or automated. Automation, to me, is an investment in your future. From the menial to the complex, automation can change your world for the better. You just need a little imagination.

For any project, one of the first questions I ask is, "Can this be systematized with automation?" My goal is to work smarter, not harder. Any time spent automating a daily task today pays you back with exponentially more in the future. Your upfront investment of even a small amount of time could equal out to days or weeks of saved time in the future.

### THE BEAUTY IN SYSTEMS

Automation is beautiful because it removes the task from your mind, but still it gets done. One of my favorite automated systems is one I set up for a small insurance firm. As a company, their biggest lead generation tool is cold calling businesses. Any time a lead says they are interested in learning about health insurance rates, the caller marks appropriate fields within their customer relationship management tool. Depending on what they select, different things happen. If a lead is marked as *interested*, a series of follow-up emails are sent out to nurture the lead on the service capabilities, history of the company, and other supplemental items. At the same time, the lead is assigned to an individual in the service department. The person is given a task to gather the census data from the company and compile a list of proposals. When the proposals are added to the CRM, the CRM picks up the proposals, inserts them into an email, and sends the email to the lead. A few follow-up emails are sent to confirm that the lead has received the information and whether they would like to move forward.

Maybe it's hard to see as described here in words, but it's magic in action. Where there used to be the need for lots of handholding and worker interaction, there is now a system that works 24/7. It's beautiful.

When it comes to work, it's worth taking time to see what can and can't be automated within your daily tasks. Automation doesn't have to be solely limited to major tasks. Frequently, it is automating the small stuff that makes the most immediate difference.

## STEP 3. HAND OFF

Out of all the steps in task-recycling, this one is probably the hardest. It's not a problem of knowing what it means to rely on other people, it's a problem of trust. Handing off a task means that you are giving something that you are responsible for to someone else. Sometimes, the person you hand it over to may not complete the task to your standards. That's just reality. Sometimes, if you want a job done right, you must do it yourself. But, doing everything yourself is becoming increasingly impossible.

### FIND SOMEONE BETTER

Tim Ferriss, in his book *The Four-Hour Workweek*, loves the idea of outsourcing aspects of your job with or without permission from superiors. Tim Ferriss talks about how it is possible to leverage outsourcing so that you are making money in US dollars, but getting work done for Rupees.

It's a fascinating subject, but one that many of us will have a difficult time implementing. While it is unfortunate, there is still a technology and language barrier that is going to impede most from being able to effectively hire virtual assistants. For me, the matter is purely economic. I don't have the funds to A/B test different virtual assistants to do my job for me. Plus, with my systems of automation, in the time that it would take for me to explain to someone in India how to do a job and wait for their response, I could have done the task 10 times. So, yes, it is true that for pennies on the dollar, you can get unbelievably quick and accurate work done for you by someone on the other side of the planet. You'll just have to weigh the trade-offs to see if it is right for you. In the meantime, use the resources around you to leverage tasks to others.

### HOW I MADE IT WORK FOR ME

I was born with a defect. This defect is an affliction that impacts around 8 percent of men and 0.5 percent of women around the world. It's misunderstood by many and causes those who have it great frustration in many aspects of their lives. The most common form of this malady is called deuteranomaly. Never heard of it? That's okay. It's better known as colorblindness, more specifically, red-green colorblindness.

Being colorblind is a big deal for me because, as a digital content manager, I deal with color daily. Whether it is balancing color in a photo, color coordinating the brand colors across multiple online platforms, or designing an infographic for a product, if I get ahold of it without a little supervision ... look out. The final product is going to be *strange*. So, in order to prevent any major moments of disaster, I outsource design tasks to one of two places. The first option is my brother. He's a talented artist. He wants to go to school to become a concept artist. So, to help him hone his craft and make a little money on the side, I throw him some design projects. The kid is good, fast, and responsive to criticism and vague direction. The second option is outsourcing to a company such as *Fiverr* (fiverr.com). On that site, I can put up an idea and designers around the world bid on the project. No matter which option I go with, I'm always happy with the result. Anything is better than the mess I would make.

## STEPS 4 & 5: TACKLE OR RECYCLE?

We've come to the last two steps of task-recycling. If the task in front of us cannot be deleted, automated, or handed off, we are at a fork in the road. On the one hand, we have the choice of directing our full attention to the task and completing it. On the other hand, we have the choice of putting the task back into the hopper to be "recycled" and run through the process again.

### STEP 4: RECYCLE

If there is no immediate need for the task to be completed, you are free to put it off. Once the task is returned to the front of the process, it will go through the steps again, but later. Like most things in life, there is a time and a place for everything. If the time and place is not now, why stress yourself out or take your eye off the things that need your immediate attention?

### STEP 5: TACKLE

The piece of work must be done. It can't wait. If all avenues of alleviating yourself of this item have been exhausted, there is nothing left but to complete it. Don't take this as a negative, though. This, usually, means that it is something you need to work on. It is likely that this is an item of high importance. This is great news. You are finally working on something that really *needs you to accomplish it.*

## A FINAL NOTE ON TASK-RECYCLING

The idea of putting some things off has a terrible stigma. It's often paralleled with laziness, unproductive behavior, and ineffectiveness. No one wants those labels associated with their work ethic (at least, I would hope not). What is important to remember is that applying task-recycling is not a tool for the lazy. In fact, *this is a tool meant for those who want to be hyper-efficacious.* Task-recycling is here to help you work on the things that will make the biggest difference in the short and long term. If you were looking for a way to put off work and watch cat videos on YouTube all day, this is not a tool for you.

## TIME-BLOCKING

In order to be efficacious, you need to be effective (focused), efficient (fast), and productive (reasonable results). Hacking the work environment, in terms of time, simply comes down to getting the most out of what you do. I have given you two tools so far: evaluating trade-offs and task-recycling. The last tool I would like to present to you is *time-blocking.*

When it comes to optimizing your time, there are dozens and dozens of strategies. For me, I had the best success at reclaiming my time, thus using it as I want, when I implemented time blocks. Time-blocking is the process of looking at your schedule and finding/creating chunks of time (any amount of time) to dedicate to certain tasks. *Successful people get the right things done.* Successful people get them done without distraction. It's straightforward.

One of my major problems, when I started working, was that I didn't have daily disciplines for my work. Don't get me wrong, I was willing to work hard and learn new things, but I lacked a system. I lacked the ability to set sail in a specific direction. Instead, my priorities and daily tasks shifted, depending on how the wind was blowing at that moment. I remember that I would wake up each day with every intention of being productive. I wanted to change the world with my skills. I'd get to work, start chipping away at projects, and then, without warning, a notification would pop up on my computer. Suddenly, my day quickly turned into a rat's nest of overlapping tasks, meetings, and chaos. I lost control. My day was swiftly placed at the whims of everyone else's design.

A successful person would never let their daily priorities fall prey to the onslaught of distractions like I did. I didn't learn this until I read the book, *The ONE Thing,* by Gary Keller and Jay Papasan. Successful people, according to Gary and Jay's research and experience, carve out times to focus on the one thing that matters most in their day (and eventually their weeks and months). This partitioning of time is called time-blocking. How ingenious, right? The secret to making the blocks of time work is that they are 100 percent distraction-free. That means no calls, texts, emails, conversations, noises, news, and, most importantly, other projects.

The blocks of time are designed to give you the ability to completely absorb yourself in whatever needs to be done. It's a time for complete focus. When I hear people complain about not getting their work done, I often hear them say that they wish they had more time. Whenever I hear that phrase, my gut instinct is to recoil and ask myself, "*Do they really need more time, or do they just need better focus?*" Often, these individuals just need more focus. The process of time-blocking gives you that ability.

Before we get into the gritty details of time-blocking, let's talk about some of the benefits. I want you to be able to see how it can change your work life, before I start showing you how to block your time.

## MORE RESULTS

First, blocking your time will make you highly effective. In fact, what you may find is that *you'll run out of things to do*. It's amazing what a distraction-free environment will do for your work tasks. Second, you'll begin to *understand what tasks matter*. This helps a lot with your ability to prioritize (trade-off evaluation) your daily activities. And, as you become more adept at prioritization, you'll start to see patterns that you can stretch out into weeks and months. You'll have control over your workdays, rather than someone else having control.

## IT'S A GAME

You may find that as you get more and more comfortable in your time blocks, you start to compete with yourself. I know I did. This may be a dramatic example (a.k.a., results may vary), but I try to complete multiple days of work in one block of time. That means, on Monday, I may try to do Tuesday and Wednesday's tasks as well, just to optimize my time and free-up my week for other activities. Sometimes, I can get an entire week of work done in a four-hour time block.

## THINGS THAT MATTER

You will become a person who wants to work on the things that matter. Because you are blocking your time, you don't want to waste it with nuanced bullshit. The desire to respond to every little inquiry and every phone call starts to slip away. When the phone rings, you get more comfortable letting it go to voicemail, or you shut down your email completely while knocking out today's major concerns. The distractions that everyone else "stays on top of" may no longer matter to you because you know your time will be better spent on things that move you and your business forward.

## PARETO'S PRINCIPLE (80/20)

As we have discussed, by the time you get to this step, you should have a very good idea as to whether the tasks you have in front of you are the most important ones. For the final step, it's time to apply Pareto's Principle and block your time. The Pareto Principle, introduced in 1895 by Vilfredo Pareto, states that in any society and aspect of life, there is a natural divide between two subsets: the "vital few," the top 20 percent and the "trivial many," the bottom 80 percent.

What I have found is that people often act busier than they are within their work environment. This is what I like to call "working for the sake of work." This is a strain of activity that everyone defaults to when they have no clear purpose. It makes them seem busy. It makes them seem like they are accomplishing something, but they are accomplishing very little.

A typical day for me looks a little like this:

| AM - *Daily Tasks* (Company A + B) | | | PM - *Administrative* | | *Growth* |
|---|---|---|---|---|---|
| 6 - 7 am | 7 - 9 am: **Comp. A** | 9 - 12 pm: **Comp. B** | 12:30 - 2 pm: **Focus Fun.** | 2:15 pm **Email** | 2:30 - 4 pm: **Learn** |
| Personal; Read | Major Tasks; Follow-up | Major Tasks; Follow-up | Automate; Eliminate; Delegate | -------- -------- | Classes; Books; etc. |

The first block is just for me. It's when I prime myself for the day. In this time block, I make breakfast, shower, and either read, or listen to positive and mentally charging things. I do this to get my mind in the right place. I learned a long time ago that if I want to have a successful day, it all starts with what I put into my body.

At first, I thought that only pertained to the food I ate, but I soon learned that if I was filling my head with terror, fear, and bad news, the rest of my day seemed to run parallel to that theme. So, I stopped listening to and watching the news, and I avoid social media like the plague. Instead, I read books like, *Think And Growth Rich,* or listen to audio clips of Jim Rohn. I've noticed that this has helped me be more creative and positive as life's little curveballs are thrown at me.

The next two blocks are where I get the majority (if not all) of my work for the day done. Each of the tasks in these blocks of time has been carefully cultivated to reflect the best ways for me to spend my time. Sometimes, these days are filled with mundanity. Not every major task is going to be life-changing, but each task is something that only I am able to do (see task-recycling). In each block segment, I turn off my phone, shut down outside communication, and keep my nose to the grindstone.

Once all the tasks for the given company are completed, I follow-up with each person who needs to know. It's important to reiterate, I follow-up *after* all tasks (looking for feedback, not direction) for that company have been done. That ensures that I am not interrupted in any way. If I finish all my tasks in a time block early, I use the remaining time to either learn something, or I shift to the next time block and begin working on the next company's tasks. Before noon rolls around, I am usually completely done with my work for the day.

The next time block is freer flowing than my morning. My morning is where I get the most work done, but my afternoon is where I give the next morning direction. I call this next block *administrative time.* As I eat lunch, I sift through any follow-up emails that have come back with new direction or input. As

I read and whittle down the requests, I apply task-recycling. I actively decide which things can be deleted, automated, and handed to others. By the time I have gone through task-recycling for each company, I am usually left with two or three tasks that I then prioritize and set out for myself for tomorrow. With my next day essentially planned, I send a few more emails to let my coworkers know that I have received their messages.

For the last hour and a half of my day, I have chosen to give myself a block of time to learn something new. This is usually where I spend time learning new skills that are in demand for my industry. These skills can range from web design to coding, to content writing, to videography, and more.

## PROTECT YOUR TIME BLOCKS

*"All good things in this world will be attacked."* – Jim Rohn

I see time-blocking as an objective good. It keeps me focused and makes sure that I get the most important things done daily. If I can complete all my major tasks before noon, it's very likely that I will consider the day a success. The worst thing that will happen to you, if you successfully implement time-blocking, is that others will see how productive you have become and start adding things to your plate. It is what is referred to as the *paradox of success.*

The paradox says: the more successful you are, the more responsibility you will be given; eventually, though, you will fail from the excessive burden and no longer be a successful person. To quote Harvey Dent from *The Dark Knight*, "You either die a hero or live long enough to see yourself become the villain." To protect you from the paradox of success, you must defend your time blocks. Here are a few ways to protect your time blocks:

## MAKE THEM IMMOVABLE

Unless there is truly an emergency or other urgent action required (such as driving your pregnant wife to the hospital), your time block cannot be changed. Your time block is immovable and unmalleable. Period. If someone needs something from you, they need to schedule time with you, at a future time and date that works with your time blocks.

## BUILD A TOLERANCE FOR EMERGENCIES

When someone comes to you with the claim that something is an emergency, resist the emotional temptation to drop what you are doing. Emergencies *are supposed to be serious.* But many people use the word emergency in order to get us to do something we wouldn't normally do. It's abuse. I'm asking you to slow down and question emergencies in the workplace. I know it's hard to remain calm when someone yells *emergency.* Yet, that's what I am asking you to do. When you hear the word *emergency* in the workplace, *pause.* Ask yourself: is this thing that is being asked of me *truly* an emergency? If need be, create a checklist of variables that must be met in order to declare something an actual emergency. What helps me to act rationally in the case of an emergency is to ask, "*Is this an emergency because someone failed to plan?*" Don't give up your plan for success to get in the shit with them.

### BE PREPARED

When I first started blocking my time, I would find little distractions to keep me from my work. Things such as getting a glass of water, finding blank sheets of paper, grabbing a snack, and checking my phone were ways in which I avoided focusing on a task. To avoid this, prep your space with all the things you might need. If you need water to help you think and work, keep a few water bottles near your desk. If you need something to chew on, buy an industrial pack of gum and leave it in a drawer. If you need a certain type of pen and paper, make sure there are plenty stored within arm's reach. Once you are in your time block, nothing should take you out of it. Remember, it's a time for 100 percent focus. You can't focus when you are distracted.

### SHUT DOWN THE WORLD

As much as it might suck, put every piece of external connection away. Turn your phone off, lock the door to your office, close the blinds, and put headphones in. The biggest distraction is going to come from other people walking into your space (virtually and in the real world). If you must use the computer, download a tool that blocks your access to certain sites during your blocked time. There are dozens out there that will keep you from going to your favorite news or social media site while the clock is ticking.

### MAKE A SIGN

Everyone has different working conditions (at least for now, but we will try to change that in the next section). Some people work in cubes, some in offices, and others work from home. If you have done everything we have talked about, but people are still coming in and bothering you, make a sign. It doesn't have to be rude or gaudy; it just must be present.

The sign can simply say,

```
┌─────────────────────────────────┐
│                                 │
│      PLEASE DO NOT              │
│         DISTURB                 │
│                                 │
│   IF YOU NEED SOMETHING FROM ME:│
│    COME BACK AT (INSERT TIME)   │
│    EMAIL ME AT: (INSERT EMAIL)  │
│                                 │
└─────────────────────────────────┘
```

## PUTTING IT ALL TOGETHER

To succeed, I need all three pieces: understanding trade-offs, task-recycling, and time-blocking. You, on the other hand, may only need one or two of these strategies. Take what you like and leave the rest. As I said in the beginning, start small. Pick something easy and master it. Then, when you are ready, move to something bigger and more complicated. The first step to hacking the normal way we work is to regain control of your time. Don't let someone else control it for you. Be the master of your days.

# Controlling: Location

When I think about the traditional office space, I see a zoo. Like a zoo, the office is designed to keep people in their special sections. Just as the lions and tigers are kept in the cat section of the park, the snakes and alligators in the reptile house, and the elephants in their safari-themed oasis, you are kept in your unique cage.

Your office is just like the zoo, even if you don't realize it. And, like the zoo, your office is a prison made to make you feel like you are in an environment that is comfortable and serene. It's total bullshit. Why do we submit ourselves to this? Why do we willingly lock ourselves in a prison that constricts both our bodies and our minds? Simply put, we've been trained to think that this is the only real way to work. But it's not.

## Open Your Cell

I advocate to both friends and family that they need to find a way out of their offices. I do not believe that humans, or animals for that matter, are meant to live in a cage. All life seeks freedom. It's why the weekend feels so amazing. It's why we say, *"Thank God it's Friday,"* and, *"Oh no ... it's Monday."* We want control over our lives. Work seems to take that control away from us. Remember, I'm not saying that work, in and of itself, is bad. I am specifically talking about being trapped in an office (or some other confined location). To achieve full autonomy and freedom, opening the cell door and escaping the confines of the office is paramount.

The goal of this chapter is to open ourselves up to the opportunity of having autonomy over our working environment. Without autonomy, without control, work and our workplace will always feel like a prison rather than a place where we can express our creativity and show our abilities.

## THREE WAYS TO WORK

In my experience, there are three ways to work. The first kind of working environment is called *office work*. It's the regular, run-of-the-mill situation that so many of us find ourselves in. For a great many of us, it's the typical cubicle environment where work begins at 8 a.m. and ends around 5 p.m. While we may have a moment of repose around noon, it's barely enough time to shovel fast food down our throats before having to rush back to our cells. It's the least fulfilling way of working and provides the least amount of autonomy.

The second kind of working environment is called *tethered work*. Many of us would happily settle for this scenario because it is a decent situation where both we and our employer compromise around our time in the office. In a tethered working environment, you spend a portion of your day or week working in the office, but another portion of your day or week working outside the office. This is an amicable situation because your employer feels like they still have a grip on you, while you get the opportunity to escape the office for at least some of the time.

The third kind of working environment is called *remote work*. This is the dream situation for both you and for me. Everything we do as remote workers is done off-site, no matter the time of day or the time of year. It's total autonomy to work and live in a way that best suits you, but also allows for you to get work completed. In order to rank the three types of work, I've made a simple chart:

| Location | Favorability | Autonomy (Freedom) |
|----------|--------------|--------------------|
| Office | Least Favorable | Negligible |
| Tethered | Favorable | Some |
| Remote | Highly Favorable | Total |

## THE OFFICE LIFE

As we continue moving forward in this discussion, I am going to use the word *office* a lot. What I mean by *office* is: *any location or situation where you must be in order to work.* This location or situation could be a literal office, but it could also be behind the wheel of a truck, a retail environment, or a lifeguard stand. It doesn't matter which environment you fall within. All that matters is that we understand that an *office* is simply the specific environment in which you are forced to reside in order to work.

### THE OFFICE

An office was a necessity decades ago. It was *the* place where news was spread, people communicated their ideas, and products went from concept to the manufacturing floor, and, finally, to market. The office has served us well over the decades and has provided us with amazing inventions, such as the Internet.

While business practices and technology have changed over the decades, the office hasn't. Sure, it got some upgrades in look and feel, but those are only superficial. Those slides (yes, elementary school, playground type slides ...), artisan chefs, and yoga instructors are just ploys to distract you from the reality that you are in an office. The *core idea* of what an office is has not changed. It's still stuffy, constrictive, and makes people resent their jobs. But times are changing.

People are coming to realize that the office is no longer a necessity but a hindrance. We are seeing this idea accepted eagerly in small startups. Because they don't have the funds to pay for a building as well as staff, they are letting their workforce do what they do best from wherever they want. Because of advances in communication and technology, we can instantly connect with anyone in the world and share our ideas. This has huge implications, all of which are positive for the worker and the employer.

### Changing It Up

Now, I don't want to spend pages bitching about the office. You know all the negatives, so there is no reason for me to belabor the point. If you are one of the unfortunate masses who is stuck in an office, there are some things you can do in order to give yourself some autonomy.

### Stuck in the Office

If you are stuck in an office, I know that there are only so many things you can do to remedy the situation without straight up quitting and getting a new job (or starting your own business).

While this may be the least desirable situation, I am not going to tell you to quit your job. As we all know, the problem with the whole "quitting your job" approach is that most of us can't just uproot our lives on a whim. We have responsibilities, bills to pay, and, maybe, a family to provide for. To just quit is too much of a change too quickly. So, what is there to do?

## START FISHING

My first piece of advice is to start *fishing*. Rewrite your resume, get a template cover letter that shows the value you can bring to a company, and start submitting your skills to other jobs that offer remote situations. There is no reason why you can't look for a new job while you are currently working. The reason I suggest this is that it is going to put you into a new mindset. Searching for a new job changes your outlook on your current job situation. It takes a dead-end, dreary job and turns it into a *temporary position* while you look for something better – something with a better work and life balance. Go to your favorite job boards, take your current title, and add "remote" to the search, and start applying for the results that show up. You will be surprised at the number of opportunities that come your way by just spending one hour a night applying to remote jobs.

## PUSH BOUNDARIES

While you are trapped in the office, seek out some creative ways to change things up. When I worked in the office, I went to the IT department and asked for two things: first, a laptop; second, access to the Wi-Fi. When they said yes, my work situation instantly changed. I was now a mobile employee – not remote, but *mobile*. Maybe I couldn't leave the grounds, but I *could* go to the employee lounge during off-lunch hours to change my atmosphere. If I needed more space to lay out a bunch of documents, I would go into an empty meeting room and shut the door behind me. Or, if it was nice outside, I would take my laptop out to the crappy, decaying picnic table that no one used. Sure, the Wi-Fi was a little spotty, but everyone else was trapped at their desktop computer, while I could take in the sun and the sound of birds singing.

## SET BOUNDARIES

To regain autonomy in an office environment where you can't escape from your desk, you need to work on instituting boundaries. Be warned, you might come off as a jerk while the boundaries are being established. One of the plagues of the modern office environment is that no one respects the workspace of their peers. We see this in all forms of communication, from email to face-to-face interactions. We bombard each other's inboxes with "urgent" messages, clog up the phone lines, and interrupt deep thought and moments of *flow* by stopping by each other's desks. It's very unlikely that any of us do these things with nefarious intent, but they do make some work tasks take longer than they need to. We need to institute boundaries.

There are three boundaries that we need to establish. The first is the *boundary of time*. Create a daily block of time where you are not going to allow anyone to disturb you. I established mine between 8 a.m. and 12 p.m. That's four hours where I shut my door both virtually and physically to my coworkers. At that time, I don't answer the phone, email, or open the door for anyone unless it is an absolute emergency (haven't run across one of those yet). During this four-hour time span, I live in a distraction-free environment. This is when I get my daily tasks done, as well as do my best thinking and planning for major projects that I am working on.

As I said, I create this boundary by shutting the door both virtually and physically. If you do not have the luxury of shutting your door, print out a sign that says something like this:

# PLEASE DO NOT DISTURB

FROM (TIME) TO (TIME)

CONCENTRATING ON A VERY
IMPORTANT PROJECT!

Hang that sign where others can see it before they can interrupt your space. Then, if allowed, pop in some headphones for a second layer of protection. You don't have to listen to anything, just have something in your ear. Now, if someone ignores your sign and comes barging in anyway, stay calm. Simply start acting like you are talking to someone on the phone:

"Yes, I can get that order in for you. When would you like that order ..."?

As you reach the end of a sentence, turn to your interrupting coworker, look them in the eye, take out one of the headphones, and say:

"Hold on Mr. Smith (the person on the phone) ..."

Then, turn to your coworker and say:

"I'm on the phone with a customer, what do you need?"

If they aren't a total trash heap of a human being, their first response should be to walk out of the room while whispering sorry. But, if they are one of those people who can't take a social cue, say something like this:

"... what do you need? Quickly, please. If you can't be quick, please email it to me."

(After a couple seconds long of a pause, start apologizing profusely to the "person on the phone").

If the coworker isn't quick about responding, just go back to talking to Mr. Smith about his order and ignore your coworker. Hopefully they will walk away and email you the thing they needed. In the response email, be sure to remind your coworker about the sign and suggest that they email you first before coming to you to make sure that no incident like that happens again.

The second boundary you need to implement is a *boundary of tasks*. This boundary is only successful if you are comfortable saying *no* to your coworkers. Harken back to your pre-hire interview. What job were you hired to do? Why were you the right person for that job? It's very likely that you were hired to do particular tasks within the company. Establishing the *no* boundary keeps everyone healthy in this working relationship. When you can say *no*, it means that you are focusing on your work and only your work – therefore giving you autonomy to be the best at whatever *tasks* you are supposed to be doing. To make this boundary work, say no.

The last way to regain your autonomy in the office is to implement the *boundary of access*. Like the boundary of time, the boundary of access is limiting someone's ability to get you off track. Business environments suffer from some strange inherent need to pull people off task. This constant pull comes in forms such as unnecessary meetings and phone calls. To make this boundary work for you, you must be willing to ask for pardon from those *off-task* activities. If there is a meeting, ask if you can get an overview of the meeting. Simply state that you are behind on your work and that your time would be better spent working on a specific project rather than sitting in that meeting. Same thing with teleconferences; ask for a write-up of the conversation. A simple way of looking at this boundary is this: if you can avoid *something* by getting a write-up of the conversation, do it. Unless you absolutely must be in the meeting, a simple one-page breakdown will keep you attuned to what is going on.

## The Tethered Life

As mentioned earlier, *tethered work* is a situation where you and your employer come to an agreement that you spend a portion of your time working in the office and a portion of your time working from wherever you see fit.

This type of working situation is probably going to be the most common form of employment in the coming decades. The reason being, it is a great mix for both parties involved. The employee can structure his or her life around work, and employers can maintain the ability to keep a finger on the employee.

For those of you working in an office, the opportunity to escape to even a tethered working situation may seem impossible, but I promise you it's not. In fact, with a little discussion with your superior, you may find it easier than you thought. I will admit, it is much easier to have a conversation about you working outside of the office if the boss likes you and knows that you are a dependable employee. If your relationship with your superior is strained in any way, they may see this as a ploy for you to do less than what you do now.

At one company I worked for, I joined the team but told the employer that I was interested in becoming a tethered employee soon. My employer told me that he would consider the situation after 90 days.

From day one of my employment, I busted my ass. I submitted plans and projects, work, and inquiries that went above and beyond my purview. For instance, the company I worked for didn't have a desire to use Facebook as a marketing channel. Being a *business-to-business* company, the Vice President of Marketing said that he saw no need to cultivate an audience there. But, to show that I was a forward thinker, I took the top four social media channels (at the time, Facebook, Twitter, LinkedIn and YouTube), and built a custom social media strategy for each one within a week.

When it came time for my review, the social media projects (and many others) were used as evidence that I was a competent and forward-thinking employee. When I asked for the tethered situation, there was only one answer my superior could give: *yes.*

## THE MEETING

Before we continue, I want to give a little insight to *the* meeting where I was awarded the tethered situation. Whether the following is sound advice for a negotiation or not, I don't know, but it worked for me, so it might work for you.

First, I called for the meeting. I didn't want to leave my boss with the responsibility of remembering or bringing up the conversation. This was important to me, so I wanted to broach the subject. Second, in the meeting, I came in timid – I wanted him to feel like I was asking for something special that only he could give me and only he could take away (a power play). Third, I told him that he could pick the days that I would come in. I made the subtle suggestion that I would prefer to come in on Tuesdays and Thursdays. I also gave the stipulation that I wanted to pick the hours. Fourth, I played the pity card. I told him that I was feeling my creativeness slip away, that I was feeling stifled and uncomfortable. I claimed that the office life just didn't seem like the right place for me. Fifth and final piece, I threw in an ultimatum. I stated that I didn't know how much longer I would be able to maintain this type of work in this type of office position (essentially threatening to quit). I knew that, to him, losing a promising employee who had been there for three months would suck. It would put him back out into the Wild West of hiring and he didn't want to do that. He hated fielding resumes and conducting interviews (which I knew – he'd told me so in my interview).

With all of that together, my tethered working situation was defined. I would go in twice a week on Tuesdays and Thursdays from 9 a.m. to 12 p.m. As a bonus, I told him that

I would come in on days other than Tuesday and Thursday if someone gave me notice; 24 hours in advance.

## THE SECRET SAUCE

The secret is to be valuable to your employer. You don't have to be irreplaceable, just be a pain in the ass to replace. If you can achieve that, you'll be amazed at what employers will do to keep you around. Remember, though, whatever situation you settle on with your employer, your tethered situation is only one conversation or major mistake away from being ripped away from you. I constantly remind myself of that truth. In order to keep my situation, I must be a damn good employee. Anything less is grounds for my boss to pull me back into the office. I don't want that.

## SPLITTING YOUR TIME

Whether you are working half of your day at home and half of your day at the office or one day at the office and the rest at the beach, it would be beneficial to split your time into two categories. In the first category, your time is spent on administrative, monotonous, and job-specific tasks. In other words, your time is spent on things that do not require interaction with other people outside of a quick phone call or email exchange. That category of work should be reserved for your time outside the office. The second category of work contains all the hands-on, collaborative work that requires intimate contact and discussion with your team. For instance, one of my duties is to shoot videos for products or demonstrations. That type of work should be reserved for when you are in the office.

## BENEFITS OF THE TETHERED LIFE

Have you ever spent an entire day at the office and felt like you weren't involved in anything important? Of course. In my experience, a tethered working situation is the antidote for those feelings. Every time I go into the office, it's like a family member is visiting from college. People are surprised and happy to see me and willing to talk to me about any ideas or issues they have come across since we last saw each other.

During my time at the office, both I and my team feel more involved in the things that we are working on together. Because our time together is precious, we don't waste it on frivolous office gossip or bullshit. We get right down to business.

# THE REMOTE LIFE

Remote work is the ultimate form of autonomy and freedom. Not having to go into the office in order to complete your work is amazingly freeing. It's the physical expression of complete autonomy. Having control over your location is like getting your license when you were a teenager. Suddenly, you were free to move about and do the things you wanted to do on *your* time. Like driving, there are still rules that you must follow, but you are no longer limited to the benevolence of someone else or stuck in the same daily conditions. You can work in a Starbucks, if you like the smell of coffee. You can work in your room in your pajamas, if you feel more creative in that atmosphere. You can even work between casts, as you bob up and down to the rhythm of the ocean.

Now, remote work has two caveats for me. First, if there is an office, I am willing to go in. There's a big difference between *having* to go in and being *willing* to go in. One is forced, the other is an expression of autonomy. If I deem that going into the office is necessary, I have no problem doing it. But, if there is no reason to go in, I'm not going to. Second, no tracking software. Companies think they are being clever and subversive when they implement systems to track remote employees. In my opinion, all they are doing is telling their remote employees that they don't trust them. So, if I work for an employer, I don't want to work under the restraints of tracking software. That tracking software can range from GPS location, to task tracking or hour tracking. If there is to be a mutually beneficial situation between myself and the company, there needs to be trust that I am going to do my job to the best of my abilities and in a timely fashion.

## BENEFITS

The benefits of working remotely are always going to be subjective to the individual. The benefits depend on what your job, hobbies, and life situation are. What you value from a remote situation and what I value from a remote situation could be complete opposites. For me, though, the benefits that I have experienced over the years have been immensely satisfying. So much so that, unless circumstances are dire, I do not believe I will ever work for a company that doesn't allow me to work remotely again. I don't care how big the salary is. I don't care how great the perks are. If I can't work where I want to, I'll say no. You may feel differently. That's fine. Remember, this is just one win condition out of three.

## CREATIVITY

As hokey as it may sound, I am not creative when I am in the office. In fact, when I am in the office, my creativity gets constrained and I start half-assing things. I like to be in a place where I can let my mind wander. Oftentimes, when my mind wanders, I stumble into ways of thinking and problem solving that I would be afraid to do at the office. Maybe *afraid* is too strong a word, but it is close to the emotion that I feel. When I start thinking *outside the box* at the office, I start to feel like I have eyes beating down my neck to get back on task the "right" way. I feel like I can't explore new, risky avenues because I don't want to waste company money or time. That feeling, that fear, is what kills my creativity.

Instead, if I am somewhere else, such as a coffee shop, I can relax. No one is breathing down my neck, watching every move I make. I can get up and take a walk outside with my journal and really think through a problem, without the fear that a superior will come along and yell at me to get back to work. I can debate, weigh options, take a step back, and formulate my plan of action so that I don't have to backtrack or correct a project that I felt rushed to complete.

## ATMOSPHERE

Like creativity, my atmosphere plays a huge role in my ability to make decisions and execute on deliverables. There are certain places I like to be in order to get certain types of work done. I know I am not the only person to think that. A wide majority of people don't see the office as *the place* where they feel most productive.

I have found there are three types of atmospheres I like in order to get my work done. First, if I am trying to be creative, I like to be in open, comfortable spaces. A few examples of these include being in a coffee shop, library, bookstore, or big meeting rooms. The space seems to expand my mind. Second, if I am trying to be efficacious, I like to be huddled over my desk. I like having everything within arm's reach. It allows me to think and act fast. I can see how everything comes together, whether it is printed on paper or covering my computer screens. Third, when I want to be contemplative and forward thinking, I like to be in places that remove the stress of work. Often, I just go to the gym and work out. That time allows for my subconscious mind to come up with answers. I usually have an *aha!* moment as I am driving back to my house. Other places that work for me are traveling out of the state, walking along nature trails, going to exhibits at museums, and so on. These places provide distraction, but distraction allows me to stop replaying the same problems repeatedly. The distraction helps me calm down in order to solve the problem.

### INDEPENDENCE

When I am not in an office, I must rely on myself to keep motivated. What I have found is that I am *way* stricter on myself than any of my bosses. My standards are higher, my work ethic is more demanding, and my accountability is more severe. To turn a phrase; I'm hard on myself. But, I think being hard on oneself is beneficial. Sure, like everything, it can be overdone, but if I am hard on myself within my time blocks (which we talked about), I can keep myself motivated and accountable for my individual responsibilities.

## PRODUCTIVITY

I believe that the single greatest benefit to an employer giving me the ability to work remotely is the amount of work I can get done. I'm not just talking about quantity. I am talking about high-quality, effective work. If I can stay in my time blocks and not have my attention be muddied by bullshit distractions (using task-recycling), I can knock out major projects. To give an example, one company I work with uses a development studio for their website and wanted to add a chat system to it. The development company wanted to charge $2,000 and eight hours for the addition. I told my boss that their quote was ridiculous and to let me do it. I implemented the chat system in 30 minutes *and* tied it into all our analytics, conversion, and marketing automation systems. Total time: two hours. Total extra cost to the company, zero. All done remotely and all in a single time block.

## SCHEDULE

This is probably the biggest selling point for going remote. You get to schedule your work and your life together. That means you no longer must take a vacation day in order to go to the dentist – or worse, take your kids to the dentist. You can enjoy a beautiful day kayaking down the river, by instead, choosing to work that night (or overtime, a few days prior). Is your family deciding to take a once-in-a-lifetime trip to Alaska? Take the damn trip and work during downtime. There is always downtime.

For me, the ability to work when it is appropriate to work, not when someone else tells me to work, is by far the best reason to go remote. It's the reason why no salary or benefit can sway me. If I need to be at the bedside of a dying relative or the birth of a child, work can fuck off. Whatever email or presentation needed to be written, it can wait. Being remote allows us to make the best decisions concerning life's important moments (trade-offs). Go remote.

# Control: Income

## Multiple Income Streams

After I achieved control over my location and my time, a new reality and way of life revealed itself to me. Since I didn't have to be in an office all day, and I could work only when I needed to work, I discovered that I now had the ability to earn money from more than one source. This idea isn't groundbreaking, of course. Loads of people have multiple jobs. What is groundbreaking is the fact that I could now perform multiple jobs seemingly at the same time.

I started off small with freelance positions. I was making a little extra money by performing odd jobs for various friends and associates. But as time moved on, I realized that I could offer the same skillsets that I was giving away for paltry sums to real companies who would pay *more* for my expertise. It was a revelation that has forever changed my life.

When I was growing up, countless people told me that the way to succeed in life was to do the following: go to school, graduate with a degree, get a good (long-lasting) job at a reputable company, start a family, and then retire from that job 40 years later. I'm sure many of you reading were fed the same or a similar story. It's the safe, predictable path of life that those who strive for mediocrity desire.

This predictable path is boring, and it abdicates control over your destiny to someone else. That's not cool. You can't depend on one source to be fruitful forever. There are countless stories of massive companies, titans of their industry, who suddenly tanked and went out of existence. If you work for a small company, what gives you any surety that your company will be around in the coming years?

## TYPES OF INCOME

There are two types of income. The first type is what Robert Kiyosaki calls *active income*. Active income is the income that you make by performing tasks for the company you work for. It's the most common form of financial intake. The second form of income is called *passive income*. Passive income comes from a source that doesn't need your constant attention, the way a regular job does. Passive income is usually generated by an asset that you own. Understanding the two types of income is very important. After you have achieved control over your time and location, it's time to start working on your fortune.

### ACTIVE INCOME

*Active income* can be defined as compensation that is earned by you based on your involvement in a task. In other words, if you must think, act, or use your time in order to get paid, you are earning *active* income. Active income is the normal way by which most people make a living. And, whether you flip burgers or work in a fancy office, if you must surrender the use of your time in order to get paid, you fall into this category of compensation.

The mentality that most people have about making more money is that they must work longer hours. That's semi-true and semi-false. Your income is based on the value that you add to a company. If you can master the skillsets necessary to add amazing value to your company, you can get compensated for it. The reason working longer hours is both semi-true and semi-false is because it depends on how you approach the value you are adding. What if you were a salesperson who spent an extra three hours a day trying to sell your widget, but were only able to sell an extra two widgets? Should you be compensated more? Sure. But what if you were able to sell 10 more widgets, but in half the time of everyone else – should you be compensated more? Of course. Both approaches add value, but one was done in a smarter way.

## PASSIVE INCOME

*Passive income* can come in multiple forms. A common form is through investment. Lots of retirees draw money every month from investments they made earlier in life. Another common form is through the renting of an asset. Some people choose to put their money into real estate and rent it to businesses and individuals. Still, there is another form of passive income where you start a small business that has automatic, monthly fees for access to some sort of value you have created. Whatever your flavor of passive income might be, passive income works around the clock. It doesn't care if you are working on it directly or sleeping. It's the best kind of income.

Passive income is in direct contradiction to the phrase, "If you want it, you have to work for it." I heard that phrase a lot in my formative years. Hell, I heard it just the other week when I was at the gym. The phrase is a common colloquialism that gets thrown around in almost every scenario of life. That phrase, though overused, is accurate. There is no such thing as a free lunch. But, is there a way to make money without having to focus all your time and attention on it? Yes. It's called passive income.

In my lifetime, I have sought after passive income in a few ways. First, I tried an online subscription for digital marketing advice pertaining to political campaigns. It didn't work. My second attempt was to invest in real estate. It has worked, but I'm not at the point where it is paying for trips around the world. If the building is functioning, every month the tenants pay, they contribute to my net worth without me having to do anything.

Most people who have a passive source of income see it as a monthly bonus that they'll use to pay themselves in the future. What I mean by that is, they take this money and save it in their retirement fund, invest in other sources of passive income (buying more rental property), or paying off past debts (student loans). The true value of an asset that pays you passively comes when the asset reaches the point where the income no longer has an obligatory place to which the income must go every month.

When the income turns into 100 percent profit, the value of your money is exponentially greater than the numbers on the check. The money can now be used to finance other parts of life – i.e. entertainment, fulfillment, and freedom. The value has transcended from numbers on a spreadsheet to complete security and financial independence.

# THE LUCK PREMIUM

If you can take control over the three pillars: *time*, *location*, and *income*, people will start treating you differently when the subject of work comes up in conversation. I can't tell you the number of times people have looked at me like a deer in the headlights when I told them that I was able to work multiple jobs, but do it from home and in less time than they worked at their one job. It's like I started speaking a foreign language to them.

If you succeed in attaining each win condition, you have unlocked a world that others only dream about. Be prepared for the backlash from others. Have a few things to say to clear the air and change the subject. If you can't change the subject, invariably, you will receive the following comment: "Wow, you are so *lucky* to have that situation."

To that I say, "Bullshit." I'm not lucky. I worked for this. I paid a premium to be this lucky. I spent years developing the skills and the value that afford me this level of autonomy. I spent nights learning new skills, sacrificed my weekends to experimentation, and innovated (at the risk of losing my own job) at work to bring in new value-added systems. Then, when the time came, I did the one thing that most people are afraid to do. I asked. I asked for the ability to work remotely, and I asked for control over my time. I feared being rejected, but I was more confident that I had developed the skills necessary to warrant my desired autonomy. I had paid my "luck premium."

Because of the skills I sought out and acquired, in the negotiation stages of employment, when I asked for the ability to work where (location), when (time), and for whomever (income), companies were happy to oblige.

So, is it luck? Not even a little. I paid a cost for this ability to have control. I did the reading, I did the experimenting, and I did the legwork in order to *intentionally* create the situation I have today. From the beginning, I never wanted to work in an office unless I absolutely had to. I did everything in my power to make sure it never happened, and I succeeded. You can too. Find a way. The more pillars you control, the more freedom you will experience.

## BECOME MORE VALUABLE

Alright. We have covered the three pillars of control that you must have to hack the normal way of working. We have concluded that you need to have control of your time, location, and income streams. In theory, this is all well and good, but now you must figure out how. The secret is, as Steve Martin said in an interview with David Letterman, to "...be so good they can't ignore you."

Having control over your location, time, and income are rare and valuable rewards in the business world. In order to receive rare and valuable rewards, you first need to be able to deliver rare and valuable skills. I know, it seems like a high bar to jump, but you can do it. I promise.

### SELF-ASSESSMENT

In the pursuit of greater value, we need to begin by looking inward. Self-reflection is how we will build a solid, principled foundation for moving forward. We need to understand where we have been in order to have a greater idea of where we want to go.

## WHAT YOU SEE

Start by simply listing out all the things you can do to add value. Don't write a resume; write a skills list. If you can edit video, write that down. If you can write marketing plans for social media, write that down. Get a well-rounded idea as to what you can do.

## WHAT OTHERS SEE

Next, go ask someone else. If you have a mentor, go ask them to do an evaluation of your skills. They can give you honest feedback without making you feel like you are being judged. If you don't have a mentor, the next best thing to do is to ask a superior (a.k.a. boss). They are a great resource because your employment is dependent on the value that you bring to the table.

It's important to get an idea of what others believe your value is because they see things from a completely different angle. For instance, I am interested in coaching at the CrossFit gym that I belong to. I believe that I have attained the skills needed to help others learn the sport. When I brought up this fact to the individual who owns my gym, he agreed that I knew the movements, but he wanted me to coach because of my humbleness. He saw my ability to empathize and be patient with others as they struggled to obtain highly demanding skills as important. It wasn't just my fundamental understanding of the movements. He believed that my humbleness would build connections that would keep people coming back to the gym.

Once you have a list from yourself and you have a list from another person (or persons), bring the lists together and see where they connect and disconnect.

## Survey the Landscape

Now that you have a general idea of the value that you bring to the table from multiple perspectives, it's time to see what other people are looking for. Even if you love the company you work for (or own), go look at what other companies want for someone with your job title, skills and responsibilities.

## What Are You Missing?

If I am a marketing manager who has focused on print media for 20 years and now things are beginning to move to a digital format, I need to know what other companies see as valuable in this new publishing medium. If I need to know how to use WordPress, or have a basic understanding of Photoshop, or of how to set up Facebook advertising campaigns, I'd better start finding ways to attain those skills. Even if your company doesn't use something like Facebook advertising now, if suddenly the demand is there, having a base knowledge of the platform and what can be done with it ensures that you will be immediately valuable. In a more negative light, if you get fired or the company you work for goes out of business, if you have kept up on emerging skills and tools, you will be more easily able to find future employment.

I know of a woman who worked for a company where the owner disliked online activity. He didn't want to sell products online, he didn't want to spend money marketing online, and he most definitely didn't want to pay for his employees to learn the skills just in case. What happened? This woman fell behind the marketing curve. She quit her job at this company and found herself in the job market, trying to apply for positions that demanded knowledge of an area of the industry she knew nothing about. Even though she had over 20 years' experience working in marketing and building relationships with major companies like Walmart, the job market demanded that any new marketing hire needed to know certain basics in the digital marketing age. She had to spend months catching up just to be considered for a position.

## PERSONAL DEVELOPMENT

Jim Rohn, in many of his seminars, said, "Work harder on yourself than you do on your job." It's a simple concept, but harder than most people think. In order to work on yourself, you must understand who you are and what you need to work on. If you have performed a self-assessment, asked others about your value, reflected on what you need to learn, and surveyed the landscape, you'll have a pretty good idea about what you need to work on with respect to your employment. Next, we need to uncover personal development outside of work.

Personal development is a two-sided coin. Some people think it means that they only need to work on things that make them happy, like hobbies. Others think it means they need to work specifically on the things that make them more valuable in the marketplace. What we are really looking for is a healthy combination of the two. Since each of us is completely different, there is no magical split that I can give you. Jim Rohn was famous for stating that to begin working on yourself, it only takes changing one thing. Whether it is eating an apple a day, reading a book, or learning how to control your emotions, each action will have a domino effect, moving to other parts of your life. It's hard, if not impossible, to do something in a vacuum.

Personal development takes time and discipline. It takes what Cal Newport calls *deliberate practice.* Deliberate practice is how we break through to new levels of competency and understanding. Most people adjust their actions and behavior until they reach a point of comfort in skills, income, or mental capacity, and then they flatline. People reach a point of complacency and comfort and then stop learning.

Deliberate practice requires that you move past that point of comfort and keep learning more. Be forewarned: deliberate practice is unbelievably exhausting. It's exhausting because it requires us to work in an uncomfortable, frustrating, and often ambiguous place. We are usually unaware of the time it will take to learn or master a concept, whether it will turn out to be worthwhile, or if we'll ever truly use what we are practicing. Deliberate practice is full of uncertainty, and uncertainty sucks.

Personal development is not a weekend project. Malcolm Gladwell, in his book *Outliers*, describes a concept called the *10,000 hours* rule. Malcolm Gladwell explains that most masters of any craft – art, surgery, septic tank cleaning, etc. – have spent at least 10,000 hours going over just the basics of their craft. The fundamentals are literally second nature to them which, in turn, allows them to explore the more complex. Be prepared to dedicate yourself to a lifetime of learning.

## Monetize Yourself

I am a firm believer in the idea that everything you do is an opportunity to monetize yourself. If you are familiar with the term *monetization*, I apologize for any confusion. We are going to use the term *monetization* a little differently. Our definition of monetization is: *the value attained from the action, skills, or expertise one collects over their lifetime.*

Nearly everything you have ever done can provide some form of monetization. Too often, we default to the idea that the only forms of monetization we can capitalize on are the moments where we have the most expertise and time invested. It is true that we will be compensated at the highest level for that expertise and time invested, but these are not the only places where you can monetize yourself.

I want to make the point that once you attain value, build it into your everyday offering. You never know when an employer or part-time job (that may eventually turn into your full-time career) may spring up because you continued to use skills that you picked up along the path of life.

Take some time to evaluate what you have done over your life and see where you can bring in such skills to increase your value. If you are looking to jump into a venture of your own, a value assessment will also help you hire people who can adequately reflect the gaps in your own capabilities.

### Again, Check the Demand

I have made it a regular practice to search on job sites for my current job title, to see what other companies are looking for in that job description. There is nothing more honest than the market. If the market is valuing other skillsets than the ones you currently have, it might be time to take a course or two online to familiarize yourself. Nearly all skills can be learned via a YouTube channel or through online courses.

Once a new skill is learned, don't hide it – tell your current employer. See if they would find it valuable to implement those new ideas in the company. If so, show initiative and take a leadership role in the implementation. If it adds value to the company (not just brings in more money, but improves process, automates mundane tasks, etc.), then ask for value in return.

It's hard to deny valuable workers the things they want. If a valuable worker is not happy, he or she can take that value somewhere else. Companies know this. If you've been keeping up with what is valuable in the market, you should have no trouble creating a position that better suits you or finding something better.

## PROTECT THE ASSET

After this journey, my hope is that I have opened your mind to a new, meaningful way of evaluating the way you and everyone else works. It is at this point where we need to actively protect the ideas so that they are not extinguished by the naysayers.

### DEFENDING YOUR THOUGHTS

Our thoughts are controlled by more than just what we come up with in our own heads. Outside influences, such as friends, relatives, and coworkers, do much to sway the way we view the world. Even those we do not know try to influence our perception with news stories, article headlines, and advertising. If we are not careful, one or more of those influences can have a dramatic influence over the value we bring to the table, both in our personal lives and at work. Things such as pessimism, over-caution, and complaining prime our minds to see the world in a negative light. They cause us to see only misery, when there is so much beauty and opportunity. These diseases of the mind can come from anywhere: friends, family, enemies, and strangers. Oftentimes, they come directly from the stories we tell ourselves. If you see value in controlling your time, location, and income, don't let others keep that away from you. Pursue it.

### Defending Your Actions

There's nothing better than doing something that brings you great joy and personal fulfillment. An example of that would be how I feel finishing this book. This was a monstrous achievement for me and one that I am very proud of. There were plenty of times when I questioned whether I should continue writing, but I kept typing away. I kept practicing, even after asking myself, "What if no one cares?"

Sometimes, you must do something for yourself. Constantly waiting for someone else to come and tell you to start or give you a good idea is a bad plan of action. One of the greatest life lessons I ever learned was that other people *do not have much planned for me.* If I want something to happen, I must plan and execute it myself. I can't wait for someone else to come and turn me on.

Lastly, the language of the mediocre and *normal* is laced with disqualifiers:

- What if ...
- I don't think I can ...
- It won't work because ...

These and other common phrases are the nails that pop the balloons of great ideas. Sometimes, you just must give it a go. Get after it. Take a risk. One of my favorite mantras is to say to myself repeatedly: *Let's find out.* Let's find out if I can run a mile in under eight minutes. Let's find out if I can get a remote position. You could live a life of safety and protection in the corner *or* you could live a life of adventure. It's your choice. The worst thing you can imagine is never actually that bad. Most of the time, the worst thing that happens is you learn something about yourself, which just adds value.

### DEFENDING YOUR EMOTIONS

This took a long time for me to get a handle on and it will continue to be a daily practice. Emotions are impulsive, unpredictable, and irrational. Defending our emotional state is *hard*. The best way I have learned to handle my emotions is to practice the art of detachment. Detachment allows me to experience the raw power of an emotion and then choose to act purposely and rationally in response to my emotions. Stop letting your emotions get the best of you. Recognize that a situation may be frustrating, take a deep breath, and then charge forward with the confidence that you know you are doing what is right for you in the long run.

Good luck out there.

# ABOUT JOHN STEVENOT...

John was born in 1990 and grew up in Cincinnati, OH. He attended St. Xavier High School and graduated with honors from the University of South Carolina Moore School of Business.

A serious student of life and business, John was an avid reader and an early adopter of working remotely and controlling one's "time and location." An exercise enthusiast and committed CrossFit athlete, John believed in working hard and living life to its fullest.

John passed away in his sleep on October 5, 2018 due to a rare and asymptomatic heart condition. The manuscript upon which this book is based was written by John in the summer of 2017.

To learn more about John Stevenot visit: johnstevenot.com